GLENCOE LANGUAGE ARTS

VOCABULARY POWER

GRADE 8

Glencoe
McGraw-Hill

New York, New York   Columbus, Ohio   Woodland Hills, California   Peoria, Illinois

To the Student

This *Vocabulary Power* workbook gives you the practice you need to expand your vocabulary and improve your ability to understand what you read. Each lesson focuses on a single vocabulary concept or on a theme that ties together the list of words in the Word Bank. You then have several opportunities to learn the words by completing exercises on definitions, context clues, and word parts.

You can keep track of your own progress and achievement in vocabulary study by using the Student Progress Chart, which appears on page v. With your teacher's help, you can score your work on any lesson or test. After you know your score, use the Scoring Scale on pages vi–vii to figure your percentage. Then mark your score (or percentage correct) on the Student Progress Chart. Share your Progress Chart with your parents or guardians as your teacher directs.

Glencoe/McGraw-Hill

A Division of The **McGraw·Hill** *Companies*

Send all inquiries to:
Glencoe/McGraw-Hill
8787 Orion Place
Columbus, Ohio 43240

ISBN 0-07-826228-3

Printed in the United States of America

9 10 024 05

CONTENTS

Unit 6

Unit 7

Unit 8

Pronunciation Guide

STUDENT PROGRESS CHART

Fill in the chart below with your scores, using the scoring scale on the next page.

Name: _____

	Lesson	Unit Review	Unit Test
1			
2			
3			
4			
5			
Review			
Test			
6			
7			
8			
9			
Review			
Test			
10			
11			
12			
13			
14			
Review			
Test			
15			
16			
17			
18			
Review			
Test			
19			
20			
21			
22			
Review			
Test			
23			
24			
25			
26			
27			
28			
Review			
Test			
29			
30			
31			
32			
Review			
Test			
33			
34			
35			
36			
Review			
Test			

SCORING SCALE

Use this scale to find your score. Line up the number of items with the number correct. For example, if 15 out of 16 items are correct, the score is 93.7 percent (see grayed area).

Number Correct

Number of Items

	1	2	3	4	5	6	7	8	9	10	11	12	13	14	15	16	17	18	19	20
1	100																			
2	50	100																		
3	33.3	66.7	100																	
4	25	50	75	100																
5	20	40	60	80	100															
6	16.7	33.3	50	66.7	83.3	100														
7	14.3	28.6	42.9	57.1	71.4	85.7	100													
8	12.5	25	37.5	50	62.5	75	87.5	100												
9	11.1	22.2	33.3	44.4	55.6	66.7	77.8	88.9	100											
10	10	20	30	40	50	60	70	80	90	100										
11	9.1	18.1	27.2	36.3	45.4	54.5	63.6	72.7	81.8	90.9	100									
12	8.3	16.7	25	33.3	41.7	50	58.3	66.7	75	83.3	91.7	100								
13	7.7	15.3	23.1	30.8	38.5	46.1	53.8	61.5	69.2	76.9	84.6	92.3	100							
14	7.1	14.3	21.4	28.6	35.7	42.8	50	57.1	64.3	71.4	78.5	85.7	92.8	100						
15	6.7	13.3	20	26.7	33.3	40	46.6	53.3	60	66.7	73.3	80	86.7	93.3	100					
16	6.3	12.5	18.8	25	31.2	37.5	43.7	50	56.2	62.5	68.7	75	81.2	87.5	93.7	100				
17	5.9	11.8	17.6	23.5	29.4	35.3	41.2	47	52.9	58.8	64.7	70.6	76.5	82.3	88.2	94.1	100			
18	5.6	11.1	16.7	22.2	27.8	33.3	38.9	44.4	50	55.5	61.1	66.7	72.2	77.8	83.3	88.9	94.4	100		
19	5.3	10.5	15.8	21	26.3	31.6	36.8	42.1	47.4	52.6	57.9	63.1	68.4	73.7	78.9	84.2	89.4	94.7	100	
20	5	10	15	20	25	30	35	40	45	50	55	60	65	70	75	80	85	90	95	100
21	4.8	9.5	14.3	19	23.8	28.6	33.3	38.1	42.8	47.6	52.3	57.1	61.9	66.7	71.4	76.1	80.9	85.7	90.5	95.2
22	4.5	9.1	13.7	18.2	22.7	27.3	31.8	36.4	40.9	45.4	50	54.5	59.1	63.6	68.1	72.7	77.2	81.8	86.4	90.9
23	4.3	8.7	13	17.4	21.7	26.1	30.4	34.8	39.1	43.5	47.8	52.1	56.5	60.8	65.2	69.5	73.9	78.3	82.6	86.9
24	4.2	8.3	12.5	16.7	20.8	25	29.2	33.3	37.5	41.7	45.8	50	54.2	58.3	62.5	66.7	70.8	75	79.1	83.3
25	4	8	12	16	20	24	28	32	36	40	44	48	52	56	60	64	68	72	76	80
26	3.8	7.7	11.5	15.4	19.2	23.1	26.9	30.8	34.6	38.5	42.3	46.2	50	53.8	57.7	61.5	65.4	69.2	73.1	76.9
27	3.7	7.4	11.1	14.8	18.5	22.2	25.9	29.6	33.3	37	40.7	44.4	48.1	51.9	55.6	59.2	63	66.7	70.4	74.1
28	3.6	7.1	10.7	14.3	17.9	21.4	25	28.6	32.1	35.7	39.3	42.9	46.4	50	53.6	57.1	60.7	64.3	67.9	71.4
29	3.4	6.9	10.3	13.8	17.2	20.7	24.1	27.6	31	34.5	37.9	41.4	44.8	48.3	51.7	55.2	58.6	62.1	65.5	69
30	3.3	6.7	10	13.3	16.7	20	23.3	26.7	30	33.3	36.7	40	43.3	46.7	50	53.3	56.7	60	63.3	66.7
31	3.2	6.5	9.7	13	16.1	19.3	22.6	25.8	29	32.2	35.4	38.7	41.9	45.1	48.3	51.6	54.8	58	61.2	64.5
32	3.1	6.3	9.4	12.5	15.6	18.8	21.9	25	28.1	31.3	34.4	37.5	40.6	43.8	46.9	50	53.1	56.2	59.4	62.5
33	3	6	9	12.1	15.1	18.1	21.2	24.2	27.2	30.3	33	36.3	39.3	42.4	45.4	48.4	51.5	54.5	57.5	60.6
34	2.9	5.9	8.8	11.8	14.7	17.6	20.6	23.5	26.5	29.4	32.4	35.3	38.2	41.2	44.1	47.1	50	52.9	55.9	58.8
35	2.9	5.7	8.6	11.4	14.3	17.1	20	22.9	25.7	28.6	31.4	34.3	37.1	40	42.9	45.7	48.6	51.4	54.3	57.1
36	2.8	5.6	8.3	11.1	13.9	16.7	19.4	22.2	25	27.8	30.6	33.3	36.1	38.9	41.7	44.4	47.2	50	52.7	55.6
37	2.7	5.4	8.1	10.8	13.5	16.2	18.9	21.6	24.3	27	29.7	32.4	35.1	37.8	40.5	43.2	45.9	48.6	51.4	54
38	2.6	5.3	7.9	10.5	13.2	15.8	18.4	21.1	23.7	26.3	28.9	31.6	34.2	36.8	39.5	42.1	44.7	47.4	50	52.6
39	2.6	5.2	7.7	10.3	12.8	15.4	17.9	20.5	23.1	25.6	28.2	30.8	33.3	35.9	38.5	41	43.6	46.2	48.7	51.3
40	2.5	5	7.5	10	12.5	15	17.5	20	22.5	25	27.5	30	32.5	35	37.5	40	42.5	45	47.5	50

Number Correct

Number of Items

	21	22	23	24	25	26	27	28	29	30	31	32	33	34	35	36	37	38	39	40
1																				
2																				
3																				
4																				
5																				
6																				
7																				
8																				
9																				
10																				
11																				
12																				
13																				
14																				
15																				
16																				
17																				
18																				
19																				
20																				
21	100																			
22	95.4	100																		
23	91.3	95.6	100																	
24	87.5	91.6	95.8	100																
25	84	88	92	96	100															
26	80.8	84.6	88.5	92.3	96.2	100														
27	77.8	81.5	85.2	88.9	92.6	96.3	100													
28	75	78.6	82.1	85.7	89.3	92.9	96.4	100												
29	72.4	75.9	79.3	82.8	86.2	89.7	93.1	96.6	100											
30	70	73.3	76.7	80	83.3	86.7	90	93.3	96.7	100										
31	67.7	70.9	74.2	77.4	80.6	83.9	87.1	90.3	93.5	96.8	100									
32	65.6	68.8	71.9	75	78.1	81.2	84.4	87.5	90.6	93.8	96.9	100								
33	63.6	66.7	69.7	72.7	75.8	78.8	81.8	84.8	87.8	90.9	93.9	96.9	100							
34	61.8	64.7	67.6	70.6	73.5	76.5	79.4	82.4	85.3	88.2	91.2	94.1	97.1	100						
35	60	62.9	65.7	68.6	71.4	74.3	77.1	80	82.9	85.7	88.6	91.4	94.4	97.1	100					
36	58.3	61.1	63.8	66.7	69.4	72.2	75	77.8	80.6	83.3	86.1	88.9	91.7	94.4	97.2	100				
37	56.8	59.5	62.2	64.9	67.6	70.3	72.9	75.7	78.4	81.1	83.8	86.5	89.2	91.9	94.6	97.3	100			
38	55.3	57.9	60.5	63.2	65.8	68.4	71.1	73.7	76.3	78.9	81.6	84.2	86.8	89.5	92.1	94.7	97.3	100		
39	53.8	56.4	58.9	61.5	64.1	66.7	69.2	71.8	74.4	76.9	79.5	82.1	84.6	87.2	89.7	92.3	94.9	97.4	100	
40	52.5	55	57.5	60	62.5	65	67.5	70	72.5	75	77.5	80	82.5	85	87.5	90	92.5	95	97.5	100

Vocabulary Power

Lesson 1   Using Synonyms

Home is a place that contains many kinds of memories–some good, some painful, some humorous, some sad. Different kinds of memories help make up our idea of home. In this lesson, you'll learn some words to use when you want to talk about what home means to you.

Word List			
anonymous	hysteria	tranquillity	wholesome
awed	lurch	valid	woe
humility	perish		

EXERCISE A   Synonyms

Synonyms are words with similar meanings. Each boldfaced word below is paired with a synonym whose meaning you probably know. Think of other words related to the synonym and write them on the line provided. Then, look up the word in a dictionary and write its meaning.

1. **perish** : die _____

   Dictionary definition _____

2. **woe** : sadness _____

   Dictionary definition _____

3. **tranquillity** : peacefulness _____

   Dictionary definition _____

4. **lurch** : stagger _____

   Dictionary definition _____

5. **hysteria** : uncontrollable emotion _____

   Dictionary definition _____

6. **humility** : lack of pride _____

   Dictionary definition _____

7. **anonymous** : unknown _____

   Dictionary definition _____

8. **awed** : admiring _____

   Dictionary definition _____

Vocabulary Power *continued*

9. **wholesome** : healthy _____

Dictionary definition _____

10. **valid** : proper _____

Dictionary definition _____

EXERCISE B **Sentence Completion**

Write the vocabulary word that best completes each sentence.

1. Despite her impressive accomplishments, the scientist kept her attitude of _____.

2. We were definitely _____ the first time we visited the Capitol Building in Washington, D.C.

3. "My heart is broken," sighed the heroine of the drama, "and I know I shall _____ before the sun rises."

4. Anyone who wishes to try out for the soccer team must have a(n) _____ certificate of good health from a doctor.

5. The Bosnian people suffered much _____ in the brutal war.

6. As the asteroid approached Earth, the people's _____ grew.

7. The engine started at last and the moped began to _____ forward.

8. The person who donated $10,000 wished to remain _____.

9. It's important that the food you eat is _____ and fresh.

10. After an especially busy day, I enjoy the _____ of lying on my bed listening to some quiet music.

Vocabulary Power

Lesson 2   Using Synonyms

As Dorothy learned in *The Wizard of Oz,* there really is no place like home. One of the reasons each home is unique is that each person who helps create a home is unique. The words in this lesson relate to the special place we call home.

Word List

alliance	indifference	simultaneous	urban
alternative	meager	taunt	varied
commence	portray		

EXERCISE A **Synonyms**

Each boldfaced word below is paired with a synonym whose meaning you probably know. Think of other words related to the synonym and write them on the line provided. Then, look up the word in a dictionary and write its meaning.

1. **taunt** : tease _____

   Dictionary definition _____

2. **indifference** : lack of preference _____

   Dictionary definition _____

3. **commence** : begin _____

   Dictionary definition _____

4. **meager** : thin _____

   Dictionary definition _____

5. **simultaneous** : at the same time _____

   Dictionary definition _____

6. **urban** : city _____

   Dictionary definition _____

7. **varied** : different _____

   Dictionary definition _____

8. **alliance** : association _____

   Dictionary definition _____

Vocabulary Power *continued*

9. **alternative** : choice _____

   Dictionary definition _____

10. **portray** : picture _____

    Dictionary definition _____

EXERCISE B Sentence Completion

Write the vocabulary word that best completes the sentence.

1. Because the two soccer games were _____, we could not watch them both.

2. "What time does the movie _____?" Jason asked, worried about being late.

3. Whether Shawna comes to the party is a matter of complete _____ to most of the club members.

4. The two countries formed a secret _____ to defend each other in case of military attack.

5. The menu choices were extremely _____. I found several things I wanted to order.

EXERCISE C Usage

Answer the questions based on your understanding of the boldfaced word.

1. Do you think a **meager** meal would satisfy you if you were very hungry? Why or why not?

   _____

2. What are some advantages to living in an **urban** setting? What are some disadvantages?

   _____

   _____

3. How would you respond if someone were to **taunt** you at school? _____

   _____

4. Name a film, TV show, or book that you feel accurately **portrays** teenage life. Why did you choose this particular film, TV show, or book? _____

   _____

5. What do you feel is a good **alternative** to settling disputes with violence? Explain your answer.

   _____

Vocabulary Power

Lesson 3   Word Parts

The main meaning of a word is contained in its root or base word. Base words are roots that are complete words. Prefixes can be affixed to the beginning and suffixes to the end of the root to change its meaning. Knowing the meanings of word roots, prefixes, and suffixes can help you make an educated guess about the meaning of a new word. In this lesson, you'll identify some common roots, prefixes, and suffixes and learn how they work together to give meaning to words.

Word List

adjourn	dramatize	mutation	precedence
anthropology	monotonous	perception	secluded
circumnavigate	mutate		

EXERCISE A **Word Association**
Read the clues. Then, answer the question.

1. The root of **mutation** comes from *mutare,* the Latin word for "change." If you add the noun suffix *-ion* to this root, what might be the word's meaning? _____

_____

2. Certain suffixes can change the part of speech of a word root. For example, *-ate* placed at the end of a root forms a verb. How would you define **mutate***?* _____

_____

3. The suffix *-ion* makes a root a noun. To perceive is "to observe." If you add the suffix *-ion,* what might **perception** mean? _____

_____

4. Prefixes can be affixed to the beginning of roots to change their meanings. The root *jour/journ* means "day." Adding the Latin prefix *ad-,* meaning "to" or "toward," creates the word **adjourn,** which probably means_____

_____

5. Some words are formed without prefixes or suffixes by combining two roots. The Greek root *anthrop/anthropo* means "human being." The root *logy* comes from the Greek word for "word" and now means "study" or "science." What is **anthropology?** _____

_____

Vocabulary Power continued

6. The prefix *mono-* means "one." The Greek root *ton* means "tone" or "sound." The suffix *-ous* forms an adjective. If someone's speech is **monotonous,** how might you describe it? _____ _____

7. The Latin word for boat is *navis.* Adding a verb suffix to this root forms the word *navigate.* If the Latin prefix *circum-* means "around," what might you be doing if you **circumnavigate** the world? _____

8. Some words have both prefixes and suffixes added to roots. The root *cede/cess* comes from the Latin for "go." *Pre-* is a prefix meaning "before," while *-ence* is a noun suffix. What might the word **precedence** mean? _____ _____

9. Another verb suffix is *-ize.* Our word root *drama* means the same as the Greek word *drama,* which comes from the word for "do" or "act." What would you do if you were to **dramatize** a story? _____

10. The root *clude* comes from the Latin word for "close." The prefix *se-* means "apart" or "away from." If a cabin is **secluded,** what other words could you use to describe it? _____ _____

EXERCISE B **Word Webs**

Choose a root, prefix, and suffix from those you learned about in this lesson. On a separate sheet of paper, draw three word webs like the one shown below. In the first, write the root. In the next two webs, write the prefix and suffix. Fill in the "rays" with as many words as you can that contain that root, prefix, or suffix. Then, exchange webs with a partner and discuss the meanings of the words you have listed.

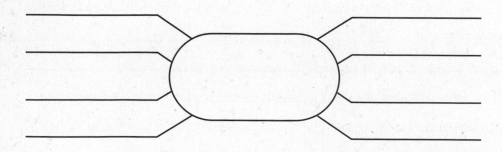

Vocabulary Power

Lesson 4   Word Families

Word families are groups of words that contain the same roots or base words. Base words are roots that are complete words. The root or base word gives a word its main meaning. A prefix or suffix combined with the root or base word gives it a different meaning. In this lesson, you'll learn words in the same word families.

Word List

belligerent	document	itinerary	levity
compel	impulsive	levitate	rebellious
doctrine	initiative		

EXERCISE A   Base Words and Word Roots

Look up each boldfaced word in a dictionary and write its meaning. Then, use the information in the dictionary entry to underline the root or base word.

1. rebellious _____

2. belligerent _____

3. doctrine _____

4. document _____

5. levity _____

6. levitate _____

7. initiative _____

8. itinerary _____

9. impulsive _____

10. compel _____

EXERCISE B   Sentence Completion

Write the vocabulary word that best completes the sentence.

1. Ms. Jackson said she was proud of the class for taking the _____ in solving the

   problem of litter around the school building and sports fields.

2. The clowns' performance ended the evening on a note of _____, very different

   from the show's sober beginning.

✿ Vocabulary Power continued

3. The television program was about the Truman _____, President Harry Truman's belief that the United States had to oppose the Soviet Union following World War II.

4. You can lead a horse to water, but you certainly can't _____ it to drink!

5. The government soldiers had a difficult time defeating the _____ forces in battle because they often disappeared into the jungle.

6. "For my final trick, I shall make my assistant _____ in the air above the audience!" announced the magician.

7. You will never convince the judge unless you are able to _____ your charges, proving that they are true.

8. Will the Grand Canyon be on your _____ for your camping trip?

9. We all felt that Rebecca was _____ when she volunteered for the committee without even knowing what she would have to do.

10. I could tell the dog was very _____ by the way it barked viciously at everyone who walked by its yard.

EXERCISE C

Answer each question based on your understanding of the boldfaced vocabulary word.

1. What are some situations when **levity** is out of place? _____

_____

2. What places would be on the **itinerary** for your dream vacation? _____

_____

3. What might be a reason some people are **belligerent?** _____

_____

4. Describe the last time you did something **impulsive.** _____

_____

5. What steps would you take to **document** a case against a factory for polluting a nearby stream?

_____

Vocabulary Power

Lesson 5   Using Reference Skills
Using a Dictionary Entry

A word and the information given in a dictionary about the word is called an *entry.* Look at the sample entry below.

Guidewords

Pronunciation spelling

preadaptation/precipitator

Entry

precipitate (pri si′ pə tāt′) *v.* **1.** to throw violently, hurl: *She addressed the difficult moral situation into which genetic engineering has precipitated modern society.* **2.** to bring about: *He precipitated a riot that led to the arrest of dozens of people.* **3.** to cause to separate from a solution: *The scientist precipitated the salt from the fluid.* **4.** to condense from a vapor and fall as rain or snow: *I hope the water in the clouds will soon precipitate as rain.*

Definition(s)

Sample phrase or sentence

EXERCISE

Use the sample entry to answer each question.

1. Which entry would you find on this page–*preach, precious,* or *precisely?* _____

_____

2. Which meaning of *precipitate* is being used in the following sentence?

   The fiery speech of the rebel leader precipitated the attack on the palace. _____

_____

3. On which syllable does the primary accent fall in the word *precipitate?* _____

_____

4. Use the first meaning of *precipitate* in a sentence of your own. _____

_____

5. Use the fourth meaning of *precipitate* in a sentence of your own. _____

_____

Vocabulary Power

Review: Unit 1

EXERCISE

Circle the letter of the word that best completes each sentence.

1. The committee voted to _____ the meeting until after the tornado alert had passed.
   a. adjourn **b.** perish **c.** taunt **d.** lurch

2. The need to rebuild some of the nation's _____ slums will be an important part of the candidate's election campaign.
   a. anonymous **b.** secluded **c.** urban **d.** belligerent

3. Kristin's _____ for Washington, D.C., included the White House, the Capitol, and the Supreme Court Building.
   a. precedence **b.** itinerary **c.** humility **d.** alliance

4. It's a shame this poem is _____ because I would love to know who wrote it.
   a. secluded **b.** anonymous **c.** urban **d.** belligerent

5. "The needs of my children take _____ over every other demand on my time," explained the employee.
   a. humility **b.** document **c.** indifference **d.** precedence

6. No matter how much they _____ Brian about his project, they cannot make him angry.
   a. portray **b.** circumnavigate **c.** taunt **d.** compel

7. Although the businessman has been very successful, his complete lack of _____ has made many people dislike him.
   a. indifference **b.** perception **c.** humility **d.** initiative

8. Ms. Dean had to _____ many of her successes in her application for the Master Teacher Award.
   a. document **b.** compel **c.** adjourn **d.** commence

9. Watch how the opossums _____ forward and then fall when they are pretending to be dead.
   a. perish **b.** lurch **c.** adjourn **d.** levitate

10. "I predict that the cells of the insect will _____ after its exposure to radiation," said the scientist in the film.
    a. adjourn **b.** dramatize **c.** levitate **d.** mutate

Vocabulary Power

Test: Unit 1

PART A

Circle the letter of the word that best completes each sentence.

1. After the Civil War, the _____ Southern states were welcomed back into the Union.
   a. alternative   **b.** rebellious   **c.** varied   **d.** simultaneous

2. Do you know which actor will _____ President Lincoln in the new film biography?
   a. portray   **b.** document   **c.** commence   **d.** compel

3. Although Woodbridge Middle School's players were much taller than we were, our volleyball team was not _____ by them.
   a. secluded   **b.** awed   **c.** varied   **d.** valid

4. The novelist had been asked to _____ her most recent best-seller, *Hope in the Dawn,* for a television movie.
   a. adjourn   **b.** taunt   **c.** dramatize   **d.** lurch

5. I found the speeches so _____ that I couldn't help yawning every two minutes!
   a. impulsive   **b.** mutant   **c.** wholesome   **d.** monotonous

6. Ola expressed _____ when we asked her which ride we should go on first, so we decided without her.
   a. humility   **b.** initiative   **c.** indifference   **d.** tranquillity

7. Because the two comments were _____, I couldn't understand either one.
   a. simultaneous   **b.** anonymous   **c.** monotonous   **d.** impulsive

8. After the young children giggled during the ceremony, their parents spoke to them about their inappropriate moment of _____.
   a. hysteria   **b.** precedence   **c.** humility   **d.** levity

9. "There's no way you can _____ me to reveal the location of the secret meeting place," thundered the hero to his captors.
   a. perish   **b.** compel   **c.** taunt   **d.** commence

10. The commission wrote that no _____ to the automobile was likely to be developed over the next twenty-five years.
    a. alternative   **b.** itinerary   **c.** alliance   **d.** precedence

Vocabulary Power continued

PART B

For each group of words, circle the letter of the vocabulary word that best fits.

1. slim, insufficient, sparse, _____
   - **a.** varied
   - **b.** meager
   - **c.** secluded
   - **d.** impulsive

2. rise, float, lift, _____
   - **a.** levitate
   - **b.** portray
   - **c.** compel
   - **d.** perish

3. good, official, approved, _____
   - **a.** simultaneous
   - **b.** belligerent
   - **c.** valid
   - **d.** meager

4. calm, peacefulness, order, _____
   - **a.** doctrine
   - **b.** alliance
   - **c.** hysteria
   - **d.** tranquillity

5. transformation, change, alteration, _____
   - **a.** initiative
   - **b.** mutation
   - **c.** precedence
   - **d.** itinerary

PART C

Circle the number of the word that is most nearly the *opposite* of the boldfaced word.

1. **thoughtful**
   - **a.** rebellious
   - **b.** anonymous
   - **c.** meager
   - **d.** impulsive

2. **happiness**
   - **a.** woe
   - **b.** tranquillity
   - **c.** humility
   - **d.** levity

3. **laziness**
   - **a.** initiative
   - **b.** alternative
   - **c.** indifference
   - **d.** levity

4. **identical**
   - **a.** monotonous
   - **b.** varied
   - **c.** secluded
   - **d.** meager

5. **finish**
   - **a.** mutate
   - **b.** taunt
   - **c.** commence
   - **d.** compel

Vocabulary Power

Lesson 6   Using Synonyms

Even the sturdiest trees sometimes lean. We are like trees—sometimes harsh winds blow and force us to lean on other people for support. This lesson provides us with words to use when exploring the ways we depend on each other.

Word List			
absurd	intimate	resolve	uncomprehendingly
arrogant	persistently	scowl	vivid
competently	postpone		

EXERCISE A   Synonyms

Each boldfaced vocabulary word below is paired with a synonym whose meaning you probably know. Think of other words related to the synonym and write your ideas on the line provided. Then, look up the word in a dictionary and write its meaning.

1. **intimate** : close _____

   Dictionary definition _____

2. **scowl** : frown _____

   Dictionary definition _____

3. **arrogant** : conceited _____

   Dictionary definition _____

4. **resolve** : decide _____

   Dictionary definition _____

5. **uncomprehendingly** : without understanding _____

   Dictionary definition _____

6. **postpone** : delay _____

   Dictionary definition _____

7. **persistently** : stubbornly _____

   Dictionary definition _____

8. **absurd** : foolish _____

   Dictionary definition _____

Vocabulary Power continued

9. **competently** : adequately _____

   Dictionary definition _____

10. **vivid** : brilliant _____

    Dictionary definition _____

EXERCISE B Multiple-Meaning Words

Many words in English have more than one meaning. Each meaning, however, is based on the meaning of the word root. The word *resolve*, for example, is from the Latin root *resolvere* meaning "to loosen," "to dissolve," or "to release." A dictionary entry for *resolve* lists many different meanings, but all of them are related to the root meaning, "to loosen." Use a dictionary to help you write the precise definition of *resolve* as it is used in each sentence below.

1. The instructor urged her students to **resolve** the mathematics problem into simple elements.

   _____

   _____

2. The negotiator tried unsuccessfully to **resolve** the dispute between management and labor.

   _____

   _____

3. Medical researchers are trying to **resolve** the chemical imbalance that triggers addictions.

   _____

   _____

4. As the debate continued, her **resolve** to support the "pro" side began to weaken.

   _____

   _____

EXERCISE C Word Association

For each group of words, write the vocabulary word that best fits.

1. proud, conceited, boastful _____

2. delay, cancel, suspend _____

3. skillfully, with ability, capably _____

4. realistic, lifelike, bright _____

5. determine, decide, settle _____

Vocabulary Power

Lesson 7   Recognizing Base Words

Words are often made up of different parts. The main meaning of a word is contained in its root or base word. Base words are roots that are complete words. Words that have the same root or base word are in the same word family. In this lesson, you'll learn to identify some common base words and explore how adding prefixes and suffixes can change the meaning of words.

Word List

acknowledge	hospitality	rehabilitate	significant
combatant	longevity	reserve	unseemly
defraud	neutralize		

EXERCISE A   Word Association

Read the clues. Then, answer the question.

1. To habilitate something is to prepare it, outfit it, or get it ready for a certain function. The word *habilitate* comes from a family of Latin words meaning "ability." What is the purpose of an institution designed to **rehabilitate** criminals? _____

_____

2. What is the meaning of the word **neutralize,** which is created by adding the verb suffix *-ize,* meaning "to engage in a (specified) activity," to the adjective *neutral*? _____

_____

3. Seemly behavior is conduct that is suitable, appropriate, in good taste, and pleasant. Our word comes from the Viking word for *fitting.* What are some synonyms for **unseemly?** _____

_____

4. The noun suffix *-ant* usually means "a person who engages in this activity." Name a famous **combatant** from U.S. history. _____

5. Synonyms of the word *fraud* include trickery, deception, and cheating. *De-* is a prefix that often creates a verb from a noun. What are some words that mean about the same as **defraud?**

_____

6. Our modern word *hospital* comes from the Latin word meaning "guest." *Hospital* was used in earlier times to mean a place where travelers could sleep and eat. What things might you do to show **hospitality** to a guest in your home? _____

_____

7. We use the common word *long* to describe both distance and length of time something exists. What comes to your mind when you add the noun suffix *-ity* to *long* to create **longevity?**

   _____

8. The word *reserve* is based on the Latin word *reservare*, meaning "to keep." What items, such as foods, would you **reserve** for an emergency such as a flood? _____

   _____

9. Many English words originate in the Latin base word *signum*, meaning "sign." Name some synonyms of the adjective form **significant.** _____

   _____

10. Unlike many modern English words, *knowledge* does not come from Latin. This base word comes from *cnawan*, the Old English word for *know*. An Old English verb form of this root is *oncnawan*. What are some synonyms for our word **acknowledge**, which comes from this Old English verb?

    _____

EXERCISE B **Dictionary Definitions**
Look up each boldfaced word in a dictionary and write the meaning. Using the information in a dictionary, underline the base word.

1. rehabilitate _____

2. neutralize _____

3. unseemly _____

4. combatant _____

5. defraud _____

6. hospitality _____

7. longevity _____

8. reserve _____

9. significant _____

10. acknowledge _____

EXERCISE C **Crossword Puzzle**
On a separate sheet of paper, create a crossword puzzle using at least eight of the vocabulary words. Then, exchange puzzles with a partner and complete the puzzle you receive.

Vocabulary Power

Lesson 8   Prefixes That Mean "not" or "the opposite of"

Knowing the meaning of prefixes can help you discover the meanings of unknown words. A large number of prefixes mean "not" or "the opposite of." Some of these prefixes are *non-, ir-, ig-, un-, mal-, anti-, counter-, contra-, de-, dis-, in-, im-, op-,* and *il-*. Be careful, though. Not all words that begin with these letter combinations have the meaning of the prefix. When in doubt, look up the word in the dictionary.

Word List

contradiction	ignoble	irreversible	nondescript
deflate	improbable	malodorous	unabashed
dismantle	inhumane		

EXERCISE A   Dictionary Definitions

Underline the prefix in each of the boldfaced words below. Base your answers on the clues. Check the definition of each vocabulary word by looking it up in a dictionary and writing its meaning.

1. **unabashed**: If you abash someone, you destroy the person's self-confidence or cause embarrassment. How might you describe someone who is **unabashed?** _____

   _____

   Dictionary definition _____

2. **dismantle**: A mantle was a kind of cloak worn during the seventeenth century, often as a symbol of authority or power. The Middle French word *desmanteler* meant "to remove a mantle." Today we use the English word **dismantle** in a general sense to mean what? _____

   _____

   Dictionary definition _____

3. **ignoble**: History shows us many examples of noble people. Name some historical figures you consider to be **ignoble.** _____

   Dictionary definition _____

4. **contradiction**: The Latin root *dict* means "to tell," and our English word *contradict* means "to tell or speak against." Adding the noun suffix *-ion* gives what meaning to the word **contradiction?**

   _____

   Dictionary definition _____

Vocabulary Power continued

5. **improbable:** Most people agree that it is probable the sun will rise tomorrow morning. What is an event you consider to be **improbable?** _____

_____

Dictionary definition _____

6. **malodorous:** Something that is odorous has a strong smell, either pleasant or unpleasant. The prefix *mal-* means "bad." What are some things that you consider **malodorous?** _____

_____

Dictionary definition _____

7. **deflate:** When you inflate a basketball or tire, you blow air into it. Describe what happens when you **deflate** a basketball or tire. In what way can a person be **deflated?** _____

_____

Dictionary definition _____

8. **nondescript:** *Describe* and *description* are based on the Latin root *describere* ("to describe"). On the basis of the meanings of *describe* and *description,* what might the adjective **nondescript** mean?

_____

Dictionary definition _____

9. **irreversible:** Many processes in life and science are reversible. Can you name some that are **irreversible?**

_____

Dictionary definition _____

10. **inhumane:** Do you have a Humane Society in your community? Many people believe that we should treat animals in a humane manner. To what **inhumane** practices might members of the Humane Society be reacting?

_____

Dictionary definition _____

EXERCISE B

Words that begin with prefixes meaning "not" or "the opposite of" appear often in newspapers and magazines. Read an article. Then, on a separate sheet of paper, make a list of words containing the prefixes discussed in this lesson. After each word, use your vocabulary skills to make an educated guess about its meaning. Then, write the dictionary definition of the word.

Vocabulary Power

Lesson 9   Using Reading Skills
Learning from Context: Definitions
The context of a word is the environment, or the other words in the sentence. You can use the context to discover the meaning of an unknown word. Look for key words and even definitions elsewhere in the sentence to help you define the unknown word.

EXERCISE

Read each sentence and use context clues to determine the meaning of the boldfaced word. Underline key words in the sentence that help you define the word. Then, write its probable meaning on the line.

1. I never dreamed that Tanya could be so **vindictive;** her demand for revenge took us by surprise.

_____

2. Tyler is **adept** at coordinating group projects; he can unify members around a common goal.

_____

3. I'm afraid that tired, old, familiar story about the farmer is very **trite.** _____

_____

4. Grandmother was a **bastion** of strength and inspiration, a rock against all the storms of misfortune.

_____

5. Hasidism is considered one of the many different branches or **sects** of Judaism. _____

_____

6. Their criticism did not **denigrate** us; they couldn't discount our project. _____

_____

7. The National Guard was called in to **quell** the violent demonstration and restore order to the city.

_____

8. The cheerleaders tried to **galvanize** the passive crowd by their lively actions and chants. _____

_____

9. The prestigious statue, standing on its black marble **pedestal,** overlooked the park. _____

_____

10. The editorial was a **lampoon,** harshly satirizing the candidate's homely features and awkward manner.

_____

Vocabulary Power

Review: Unit 2

EXERCISE A

For each group of words, circle the letter of the vocabulary word that belongs.

1. clear, bright, sharp, _____
   a. absurd   **b.** vivid   **c.** improbable   **d.** trite

2. retain, keep, book, _____
   a. reserve   **b.** neutralize   **c.** resolve   **d.** quell

3. dull, boring, uninteresting, _____
   a. absurd   **b.** nondescript   **c.** unabashed   **d.** adept

4. cruel, mean, vicious, _____
   a. arrogant   **b.** unabashed   **c.** inhumane   **d.** unseemly

5. cheat, swindle, steal, _____
   a. postpone   **b.** reserve   **c.** dismantle   **d.** defraud

EXERCISE B

Circle the letter of the word that best completes the sentence.

1. The league was forced to _____ all games because of the heat wave.
   a. rehabilitate   **b.** deflate   **c.** galvanize   **d.** postpone

2. Our basketball coach hoped that our smaller, faster players would _____ the other team's
   taller players.
   a. neutralize   **b.** resolve   **c.** lampoon   **d.** defraud

3. Alan felt that he would first have to _____ the lawnmower to understand how it worked.
   a. acknowledge   **b.** rehabilitate   **c.** dismantle   **d.** galvanize

4. Sean argued so _____ for going to the movie that I finally agreed to go.
   a. improbably   **b.** unseemly   **c.** persistently   **d.** uncomprehendingly

5. The prison program tried to _____ criminals and prepare them for life outside of prison.
   a. denigrate   **b.** rehabilitate   **c.** postpone   **d.** deflate

Vocabulary Power

Test: Unit 2

PART A

Circle the letter of the word that best fits.

1. Which word would describe the way you'd feel if you found yourself in a ridiculous situation?
   - **a.** absurd
   - **b.** vivid
   - **c.** nondescript
   - **d.** vindictive

2. How would someone probably respond if you called him or her an unflattering name?
   - **a.** resolve
   - **b.** defraud you
   - **c.** scowl at you
   - **d.** reserve you

3. Up the down stairs, cool heat, and going under an overpass are examples of _____.
   - **a.** hospitality
   - **b.** combatants
   - **c.** longevity
   - **d.** contradiction

4. How would you be doing a task if you had no idea how to proceed?
   - **a.** persistently
   - **b.** uncomprehendingly
   - **c.** competently
   - **d.** improbably

5. A tortoise that lives for one hundred years is an example of _____.
   - **a.** longevity
   - **b.** hospitality
   - **c.** a pedestal
   - **d.** a contradiction

6. You would probably _____ a meeting if not enough people could show up for it.
   - **a.** rehabilitate
   - **b.** dismantle
   - **c.** postpone
   - **d.** lampoon

7. Stealing, lying, and cheating are examples of what kind of conduct?
   - **a.** trite
   - **b.** arrogant
   - **c.** irreversible
   - **d.** ignoble

8. To what kind of friend would you tell a special secret?
   - **a.** an unseemly one
   - **b.** a vindictive one
   - **c.** an inhumane one
   - **d.** an intimate one

9. What would you expect when you check into an expensive resort hotel?
   - **a.** a bastion
   - **b.** hospitality
   - **c.** longevity
   - **d.** a scowl

10. You would most likely remember a _____ dream.
    - **a.** nondescript
    - **b.** malodorous
    - **c.** vivid
    - **d.** trite

11. How would someone who is well trained in lifesaving techniques perform the job of lifeguard?
    - **a.** uncomprehendingly
    - **b.** persistently
    - **c.** competently
    - **d.** improbably

12. Which word is an antonym for, or the opposite of, "blow up"?
    - **a.** quell
    - **b.** deflate
    - **c.** dismantle
    - **d.** reserve

Vocabulary Power *continued*

13. Which of the following words describes the way a barnyard probably smells to most people?
    a. absurd   **b.** nondescript   **c.** unabashed   **d.** malodorous

14. Having your appendix taken out is a procedure like this.
    a. irreversible   **b.** unseemly   **c.** inhumane   **d.** trite

15. Society will gain if it can _____ people sent to prison for committing crimes.
    a. dismantle   **b.** intimate   **c.** neutralize   **d.** rehabilitate

PART B

Circle the letter of the word that best fits with the others.

1. decide, determine, conclude, _____
   a. postpone   **b.** resolve   **c.** defraud   **d.** quell

2. soldier, sailor, marine, _____
   a. sect   **b.** contradiction   **c.** combatant   **d.** pedestal

3. improper, impolite, unsuitable, _____
   a. improbable   **b.** inhumane   **c.** arrogant   **d.** unseemly

4. poised, unashamed, confident, _____
   a. unabashed   **b.** intimate   **c.** ignoble   **d.** nondescript

5. conceited, proud, stuck-up, _____
   a. absurd   **b.** arrogant   **c.** unabashed   **d.** significant

Vocabulary Power

Lesson 10   Using Synonyms

Sometimes it's easy to tell when you reach an important turning point. Other times you may not know you have arrived at a crossroad until later. Either way, the choices people make always have consequences. Taking one road always leads to a destination, even if you're not sure where you're going. In this lesson, you'll learn words that relate to making decisions.

Word List

abundant	lapse	serene	testimony
complex	loiter	summon	verbal
enclose	plight		

EXERCISE A   **Synonyms**

Each boldfaced word below is paired with a synonym whose meaning you probably know. Think of other words related to the synonym and write your ideas on the line provided. Then, look up the boldfaced word in a dictionary and write its meaning.

1. **lapse** : decline _____

   Dictionary definition _____

2. **serene** : calm _____

   Dictionary definition _____

3. **summon** : call _____

   Dictionary definition _____

4. **plight** : predicament _____

   Dictionary definition _____

5. **complex** : complicated _____

   Dictionary definition _____

6. **abundant** : plentiful _____

   Dictionary definition _____

7. **enclose** : surround _____

   Dictionary definition _____

8. **verbal** : associated with words _____

   Dictionary definition _____

Vocabulary Power *continued*

9. **testimony** : statement _____

   Dictionary definition _____

10. **loiter** : stand around _____

   Dictionary definition _____

EXERCISE B Word Association
Cross out the word that does not belong with the others.

1. plight, problem, testimony, jam

2. knotty, complex, complicated, abundant

3. summon, trap, coop, enclose

4. written, verbal, serene, spoken

5. linger, lapse, delay, loiter

EXERCISE C Context Clues
Answer each question, based on your knowledge of the boldfaced word.

1. In what **plight** might travelers in the desert find themselves? _____

   _____

2. What is one technique you use to stay **serene** before a stressful event? _____

   _____

3. Why might store owners not like people to **loiter** around their entrances? _____

   _____

4. What is the most **complex** meal you have ever prepared? What made it so complex? _____

   _____

5. Describe a time when you had a **lapse** of concentration. What happened as a result? _____

   _____

Vocabulary Power

Lesson 11   Prefixes That Tell Where

Knowing the meaning of prefixes can help you discover the meanings of unknown words. A number of prefixes tell "where" and provide a meaning that relates to location. Some of these prefixes are *ab-*, *ad-*, *de-*, *ex-*, *in-*, *inter-*, *intra-*, *per-*, *sub-*, and *trans-*. In this lesson, you'll learn words that use five of these "where" prefixes. Be careful, though. Not all words that begin with these letter combinations have the meaning of the prefix. When in doubt, look up the word in a dictionary.

Word List			
abdicate	intervention	perforate	transfix
abduction	intramural	perpetual	transmission
intermediate	intravenous		

EXERCISE A   Word Association

Underline the prefix in each of the boldfaced words. Answer the question. Then, check the definition of the boldfaced word in a dictionary and write its meaning.

1. **transmission:** The prefix *trans-* is a "where" prefix that means "across" or "through." The Latin root *miss* means "send." What might be the meaning of these two word elements when combined with the noun suffix *-ion?* Why is this word also used to name an important part of an automobile?

   _____

   Dictionary definition _____

2. **transfix:** The root *fix* comes from the Latin word meaning to "fasten" or "pierce." If you experience something that has the power to **transfix** you, what words could you use to describe the experience?

   _____

   Dictionary definition _____

3. **abdicate:** Another prefix that relates to location is *ab-*, which means "from." The root *dic*, the same one used in such words as *dictate, diction,* and *predict,* means "tell." What would a king be doing if he were to **abdicate** his throne? _____

   Dictionary definition _____

4. **abduction:** Another common Latin root, *duc*, means "to lead" and is used in words like *conduct* and *conductor.* If police are investigating the **abduction** of a child, what is another word for this crime?

   _____

   Dictionary definition _____

Vocabulary Power *continued*

5. perpetual: The "where" prefix *per-* has the meaning of "through" or "throughout." The prefix can be combined with a root that means "to go to." What might be the meaning of the adjective **perpetual** formed by this root and prefix? _____

Dictionary definition _____

6. perforate: The Latin root *forare* means "to bore" or "to drill." If a machine is designed to **perforate** something, what is it probably doing? _____

Dictionary definition _____

7. intermediate: The Latin prefix *inter-* means "between," while the root *med, medi* means "middle." If something is located in an **intermediate** position, where would you find it? _____

_____

Dictionary definition _____

8. intervention: The root *ven/veni* comes from the Latin word for "come." What are some situations in which a police officer might take part in an **intervention?** _____

_____

Dictionary definition _____

9. intramural: A similar prefix, *intra-,* means "within," "during," or "inside of." *Mur* is a Latin root meaning "wall." When you play an **intramural** sport, whom are you playing against? How does this kind of activity differ from interscholastic sports? _____

_____

Dictionary definition _____

10. intravenous: The English word *vein* comes from the Latin word *vena. Venous* is the adjective form. If you receive an **intravenous** injection rather than a shot in a muscle or just under your skin, where does the needle go? _____

Dictionary definition _____

EXERCISE B Finding "Where" Prefixes

Words that begin with prefixes that tell "where" appear often in newspapers and magazines. Read a newspaper or magazine article. Then, on a separate sheet of paper, make a list of the words you find containing the prefixes discussed in this lesson. After each word, use your vocabulary skills to make an educated guess about its meaning. Then, use a dictionary to write its definition.

Vocabulary Power

Vocabulary Power

Lesson 12   Greek Word Roots

In this lesson, you'll learn ten useful English words based on Greek roots. Knowing the meanings of Greek roots can help you make an educated guess about the meaning of a new word. Sometimes, however, the exact meaning of the new word isn't clear from the root. It's always safer to look up new words in a dictionary.

Word List

apathetic	hydrophobia	phobia	phonograph
autonomous	pathos	phonetics	sophisticated
autopsy	philosophical		

EXERCISE A   Word Association

Read the clues and answer the question. Then, look up the boldfaced word's definition in a dictionary and write the definition on the second line.

1. *Phon, phono* is a common Greek root that means "sound," "speech," or "voice." Adding a suffix to this root creates the word *phonetics.* What subject do you think is studied in the science of **phonetics?**

   _____

   Dictionary definition _____

2. Sometimes words are formed by joining two roots and their meanings, rather than by adding a prefix or suffix to a root. What is the literal meaning of **phonograph,** a word created by joining the Greek root *graph* "write" to *phono?* What is another name for this machine? _____

   Dictionary definition _____

3. Since the Greek root *aut/auto* means "self" or "same" and *nomos* means "law," what is an **autonomous** country? _____

   Dictionary definition _____

4. *Opt,* a root that comes from the Greek word for "sight," is used in our words *optical* and *optician.* The word **autopsy** is formed by adding the prefix *auto-* to the root *opt.* Why might a doctor perform an **autopsy** on a dead body?

   _____

   Dictionary definition _____

5. **Phobia** is a Greek root that means "fear." We use the same word in English to describe a certain kind of feeling about a specific object or idea. How would you describe this feeling?

   _____

   Dictionary definition _____

Vocabulary Power continued

6. You probably know the Greek root *hydr/hydro* from such words as *hydraulic, hydrogen, hydro-electric,* and *hydrant.* From what special fear does someone with **hydrophobia** suffer?

_____

Dictionary definition _____

7. "Suffering" or "feeling" is the meaning of the Greek root *path/patho.* If a work of art like a painting, poem, or play creates **pathos** in the people who experience it, what might they be feeling?

_____

Dictionary definition _____

8. The meaning of the root and the part of speech may be changed by the addition of different prefixes and suffixes. The prefix *a-* is a negative prefix, while the suffix *-ic* forms an adjective. How might you describe someone who is **apathetic?** _____

Dictionary definition _____

9. The Greek root *soph* means "wise." In what way is someone who is **sophisticated** also wise?

_____

Dictionary definition _____

10. *Phil/philo* is a Greek root meaning "loving" or "having a special fondness or interest in." When the roots *philo* and *soph* are combined, the new word *philosophical* is formed. What does a **philosophical** person love? _____

Dictionary definition _____

EXERCISE B **Sentence Completion**
Write the word that best completes the sentence.

1. It's very hard to get students to serve on committees because so many people are _____ about school issues.

2. Darcie's mom let us play some of the old _____ records she has kept from the 1960s.

3. All of my conversations with Scott are very _____ – we're both voracious readers.

4. A special tutor helped Jason overcome his _____ of mathematics and attain a B+ on the exam.

5. The representative from the territory argued that his people deserved to be a(n) _____ nation.

Vocabulary Power

Lesson 13   Suffixes That Form Nouns

When a suffix is added to a word or root, the word's use in the sentence is often changed. Some common suffixes that change a word or root into a noun are *-ant* or *-ent, -ate, -oid, -ory, -tude, -ite,* and *-an* or *-ian.* Some noun suffixes refer to the person who performs an activity, while others mean the activity itself. For example, the verb *act* ("to perform") may be changed to *actor* ("a person who performs") or *action* ("performance"). In this lesson, you'll explore how noun suffixes are used to create different words.

> **Word List**
>
> | | | | |
> |---|---|---|---|
> | adherent | dormitory | lavatory | occupant |
> | authoritarian | gratitude | mandate | urbanite |
> | certitude | humanoid | | |

EXERCISE **Word Association**

Read the clues and answer the question. Then, look up the boldfaced word's definition in a dictionary and write the definition on the second line.

1. As a noun suffix, *-ate* means "function," "office," or "rank." Our word *mandate* comes from the Latin

   word *manus,* meaning "hand," and *mandare,* meaning "to entrust." If a court delivers a **mandate,**

   what is it doing? _____

   Dictionary definition _____

2. To adhere to something means "to follow," "to give support to," or "to believe in." The noun suffix

   -ent, like the more common suffix *-er,* means "one who." Name a religion, political party, or other

   belief of which you are an **adherent.** _____

   Dictionary definition _____

3. The noun suffix *-ant* is a variation of *-ent.* To occupy something is to live in it or be located in it.

   Who is the **occupant** of the desk to your right? Of the home next to yours? _____

   _____

   Dictionary definition _____

4. The noun suffix *-ory* comes from Latin and means "place for." This suffix is used with many differ-

   ent words, some of which are Latin roots. The Latin root *dorm* means "to sleep." What is the

   main purpose of a **dormitory?** _____

   Dictionary definition _____

Vocabulary Power *continued*

5. The Latin root *lav* means "to wash." What activity occurs in a **lavatory**? _____

_____

Dictionary definition _____

6. Another noun suffix you may be familiar with is *-oid,* which means "resembling" or "similar to." If

aliens from outer space are described as **humanoid,** what features might the aliens have?

_____

Dictionary definition _____

7. Another noun suffix is *-tude,* which means "the state of being" or "the condition of." Many English

words are based on the Latin root *grat*, meaning "thankful." How would you define the noun **gratitude?**

_____

Dictionary definition _____

8. Words like *certain, certify,* and *certainly* are based on the Latin root *cernere* meaning "to decide"

or "to judge." Another word that uses this root is **certitude**. What might be its meaning? _____

_____

Dictionary definition _____

9. A common noun suffix is *-an* or *-ian.* It means "being one of," "related to," or "a member of." The

root *author* comes from the Latin word meaning "power." What words might you use to describe

a leader who is an **authoritarian?** _____

_____

Dictionary definition _____

10. One more common noun suffix is *-ite.* It means "someone who is a follower of" or "a resident of." You

can find this suffix attached to many different words. One word is **urbanite,** based on the Latin root *urb,*

meaning "city." In your opinion, what are some advantages and disadvantages of being an **urbanite?**

_____

Dictionary definition _____

Vocabulary Power

Lesson 14:   Using Reference Skills
Using a Thesaurus: Synonyms

A thesaurus (from the ancient Greek word for *treasure*) is a useful reference work that lists synonyms (and often antonyms) for thousands of words. The synonyms vary slightly in meaning, and the listing is designed to help you choose just the right word. Some thesauruses list the words in an index. A reference number guides you to a listing in the main part of the thesaurus. This is the way the most famous thesaurus, originally compiled by Peter Roget (row-ZHAY) in the mid-nineteenth century, is organized. Other thesauruses arrange the words in alphabetical order. The entry word is followed by a list of synonyms and, sometimes, antonyms (opposites). In this lesson, you'll get practice in using a thesaurus to find synonyms.

EXERCISE

Below you'll find some entries from a thesaurus. Study the entries. Then, answer the questions.

> **assail** *v.* ambush, assault, attack, batter, beat, invade, raid, storm, strike, wallop, waylay
> **demure** *adj.* bashful, gentle, innocent, modest, quiet, reserved, shy, timid
> **impediment** *n.* affliction, bar, barrier, blockage, difficulty, flaw, obstacle, obstruction, snag
> **lucid** *adj.* clear, clear-cut, coherent, direct, easy, intelligible, logical, simple, understandable

1. Which synonyms for **demure** seem to you to express a positive feeling? _____

    _____

    A negative feeling? _____

    _____

    Explain your answers. _____

    _____

2. Which synonym for **assail** seems to you to be the strongest in its feeling? _____

    _____

    Which seems the mildest? _____

3. Suppose you are having trouble deciding whether to use "coherent" or "intelligible" as a synonym

    for **lucid.** How would you find out exactly how the two words differ in meaning?_____

    _____

4. **Impediment** appears here as a noun. The verb form of this word is *impede.* Based on this

    thesaurus entry, what might be some synonyms for the verb *impede?* _____

    _____

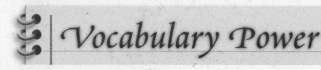

Vocabulary Power

Review: Unit 3

EXERCISE A

Circle the word that does not belong with the others.

1. follower, believer, supporter, authoritarian

2. plentiful, perpetual, in good supply, ample

3. adherent, free-standing, self-governing, independent

4. punch, drill, bore, enclose

5. problem, difficulty, mandate, jam

EXERCISE B

Circle the word in parentheses that best completes the sentence.

1. After losing the election, Margo lost interest in politics and became (abundant, serene, apathetic).

2. The figure skater glided in a (serene, perpetual, verbal) way across the ice.

3. Throwing pies in people's faces is not the most (autonomous, intermediate, sophisticated) kind of comedy, but it can be funny anyway.

4. Middle or (intermediate, complex, perpetual) school comes between elementary and high school.

5. The old woman expressed (certitude, gratitude, hydrophobia) to the firefighters who had rescued her.

6. The king decided to (summon, transfix, perforate) all of the nobles in the kingdom to discuss the crisis.

7. Some coaches are relaxed and easy with their team members, while others can be quite (intramural, intermediate, authoritarian), putting in place many rules and expecting obedience.

8. The inventor claimed to have invented a(n) (perpetual, intravenous, abundant) motion machine, one that would run forever without needing a source of energy.

9. The farmer built a new corral to (perforate, enclose, summon) his sheep and goats.

10. The governor followed the (abduction, intervention, mandate) of voters and signed the bill into law.

Vocabulary Power

Test: Unit 3

PART A

Circle the letter of the word that best completes the sentence.

1. Troy's score on the _____ test section was higher than that on the mathematics section.
   a. verbal   **b.** intramural   **c.** autonomous   **d.** apathetic

2. The veterinarian gave the lamb an _____ injection of vitamins.
   a. intervention   **b.** intermediate   **c.** intravenous   **d.** intramural

3. The advertisement was addressed to "_____," so I just tossed it in the wastebasket.
   a. Adherent   **b.** Abundant   **c.** Humanoid   **d.** Occupant

4. Mozart's opera _____ *from the Seraglio* is about an attempted kidnapping that takes place in a Turkish sultan's palace.
   a. *Abduction*   **b.** *Intervention*   **c.** *Transmission*   **d.** *Plight*

5. Greg lost the chess game because he had a short _____ of concentration and made a single bad move.
   a. plight   **b.** lapse   **c.** mandate   **d.** certitude

6. The mountain sunset was so beautiful that it had the power to _____ everyone in our hiking group.
   a. transfix   **b.** enclose   **c.** perforate   **d.** abdicate

7. A knowledge of _____ can be a great help when you try to learn a foreign language.
   a. hydrophobia   **b.** transmission   **c.** certitude   **d.** phonetics

8. I wish people wouldn't _____ on the corner of our block.
   a. abdicate   **b.** loiter   **c.** summon   **d.** enclose

9. The _____ of the trapped miners captured the sympathy of the entire country.
   a. mandate   **b.** phobia   **c.** lapse   **d.** plight

10. Terence's sprained ankle was so severe that the quick _____ of a doctor was required.
    a. transmission   **b.** pathos   **c.** intervention   **d.** gratitude

Vocabulary Power continued

PART B

Circle the letter of the word that is most nearly an antonym, or the opposite, of the boldfaced word.

1. **excitable**
   a. perpetual   b. philosophical   c. autonomous   d. intravenous

2. **doubt**
   a. pathos   b. gratitude   c. intervention   d. certitude

3. **simple**
   a. complex   b. intermediate   c. abundant   d. verbal

4. **keep**
   a. transfix   b. loiter   c. enclose   d. discard

5. **affectionate**
   a. apathetic   b. perpetual   c. autonomous   d. abundant

PART C

Circle the letter of the word that best matches each clue.

1. People buy certain products when a celebrity gives one of these.
   a. a phonograph   b. a testimony   c. a mandate   d. certitude

2. This is something that can happen to people only after they are dead.
   a. autopsy   b. intervention   c. abduction   d. hydrophobia

3. Without this, you would not be able to drive a car anywhere.
   a. an adherent   b. a phobia   c. a testimony   d. a transmission

4. A New Yorker is one, and so is a Chicagoan.
   a. urbanite   b. authoritarian   c. adherent   d. occupant

5. In this, you'd find many beds.
   a. testimony   b. lavatory   c. dormitory   d. mandate

Vocabulary Power

Lesson 15   Using Synonyms

The desire to make mischief is widespread, especially among children. What do you think makes people eager to play tricks on others? The words in the list below relate to such mischief.

Word List

comply	invigorating	pact	rogue
haggle	invincible	reckless	vibrant
imply	obstruction		

EXERCISE A **Synonyms**

Each boldfaced word below is paired with a synonym whose meaning you probably know. Think of other words related to the synonym and write them on the line provided. Then, look up the boldfaced word in a dictionary and write its definition.

1. **pact** : agreement _____

   Dictionary definition _____

2. **vibrant** : spirited _____

   Dictionary definition _____

3. **haggle** : bargain _____

   Dictionary definition _____

4. **comply** : obey _____

   Dictionary definition _____

5. **invincible** : unconquerable _____

   Dictionary definition _____

6. **obstruction** : obstacle _____

   Dictionary definition _____

7. **rogue** : rascal _____

   Dictionary definition _____

8. **imply** : suggest _____

   Dictionary definition _____

Vocabulary Power continued

9. **reckless** : heedless _____

   Dictionary definition _____

10. **invigorating** : energizing _____

    Dictionary definition _____

EXERCISE B   Context Clues

Write the vocabulary word that could describe each example.

1. an agreement between two countries to limit nuclear weapons _____

2. a person begs, causes mischief, and then skips town _____

3. someone running out into a busy intersection without looking _____

4. city streets full of people walking, talking, and having a good time _____

5. to follow the instructions of a boss at work _____

6. a brisk walk on a frosty winter morning _____

7. a plastic toy stuck in a drainpipe and slowing the flow of water _____

8. using your tone of voice to suggest that something is wrong _____

9. to negotiate the price of an item at a yard sale _____

10. how a chess player feels who has won the last hundred games he has played _____

EXERCISE C   Word Association

Circle the word that does not belong with the others.

1. alive, invigorating, unresponsive, vibrant

2. embezzle, negotiate, barter, haggle

3. suggest, deduce, mean, imply

4. mighty, invincible, unconquerable, vulnerable

5. obstruction, impediment, passage, barrier

EXERCISE D   Description

Using one or more of the vocabulary words, describe mischief or a trick you've experienced, observed, or read about.

Name _____ Date _____ Class _____

Vocabulary Power

Lesson 16   Using Definitions

The word *fantastic* means "out of this world" and comes from the Greek word *phantastikos,* meaning "producing mental images." Fantastic (or fantasy) stories might take place at any time. What sets fantasy stories apart from other kinds of stories are imaginary settings or supernatural events. The words in this list relate to the fantastic.

Word List

dumbfounded	gauge	novel	revive
ford	illuminate	remote	unsound
frugal	jut		

EXERCISE A Definition Clues

Each example below contains a clue about the meaning of the boldfaced word. Use the clue to guess the word's likely meaning. Then, look up the word in a dictionary and write its meaning.

1. **novel** : making a dress out of newspaper _____

   Dictionary definition _____

2. **remote** : a cabin on a lonely mountain in Alaska _____

   Dictionary definition _____

3. **ford** : ride a horse across a stream at a shallow place _____

   Dictionary definition _____

4. **illuminate** : explain the style of a painting _____

   Dictionary definition _____

5. **gauge** : measure yesterday's rainfall at 1.5 inches _____

   Dictionary definition _____

6. **unsound** : a floor that is rotten and has many holes _____

   Dictionary definition _____

7. **jut** : what a protruding cliff on a mountain face might do _____

   Dictionary definition _____

8. **dumbfounded** : response to unbelievable news _____

   Dictionary definition _____

Vocabulary Power *continued*

9. **frugal** : person who spends money only on necessary items _____

   Dictionary definition _____

10. **revive** : bring back a midnight movie series _____

    Dictionary definition _____

EXERCISE B Multiple-Meaning Words

Many words in English have more than one meaning. Each meaning, however, is based on the meaning of the word root. The word *remote,* for example, is from the Latin *remotus,* past participle of *removere,* meaning "to remove." A dictionary entry for *remote* lists many different meanings, all of which are related to the root meaning, "to remove." Use a dictionary to help you write the precise definition of *remote* as it is used in each sentence below.

1. King Arthur and the Knights of the Round Table are legendary figures from the **remote** past.

   Dictionary definition _____

2. We encountered the recluse in a **remote** cabin in the hills.

   Dictionary definition _____

3. **Remote** sensing equipment enables police in helicopters to spot fugitives on the run.

   Dictionary definition _____

4. An acorn is cupped in a hardened structure **remote** from the nut.

   Dictionary definition _____

5. Jason realized that he had only a **remote** possibility of winning the track meet.

   Dictionary definition _____

6. The evening-news producers inserted a **remote** from the hurricane area.

   Dictionary definition _____

7. We found the long-lost television **remote** control under the sofa cushions.

   Dictionary definition _____

Vocabulary Power

Lesson 17 Prefixes That Tell When

A prefix is a word part attached at the beginning of a word or root. The prefix *re-,* for example, means "again" or "back"; *pre-* means "before" or "in front of." Adding a prefix to a word or root modifies its meaning. For instance, the word *re-create* means "create again," and the word *pretreat* means "treat before." Recognizing these two prefixes that tell *when* can often help you figure out a word's meaning.

Word List

precaution	premeditated	recur	regenerate
precondition	reconstruct	refurbish	reintegrate
prefix	recount		

EXERCISE A **Prefixes**

Use the meaning of the prefix and the information given about the base word or root to supply a possible meaning for each word. Then, look up the word in a dictionary and write its definition.

1. The root *count* means "relate." **Recount** might mean _____

_____

Dictionary definition _____

2. A condition is a state of being. **Precondition** might mean _____

_____

Dictionary definition _____

3. *Construct* means "build." **Reconstruct** might mean _____

_____

Dictionary definition _____

4. *Meditate* means "ponder" or "plan." **Premeditated** might mean _____

_____

Dictionary definition _____

5. *Fix* means "stabilize" or "appoint." **Prefix** might mean _____

_____

Dictionary definition _____

Vocabulary Power continued

6. *Furbish* means "clean" or "polish." **Refurbish** might mean _____

_____

Dictionary definition _____

7. *Integrate* means "unite." **Reintegrate** might mean _____

Dictionary definition _____

8. *Caution* comes from the Latin infinitive *cavere,* meaning "to be on guard." **Precaution** might mean

_____

Dictionary definition _____

9. *Generate* means "produce." **Regenerate** might mean _____

_____

Dictionary definition _____

10. The root *cur* comes from the Latin word for "run." **Recur** might mean_____

_____

Dictionary definition _____

EXERCISE B Usage

Complete each sentence with the correct vocabulary word.

1. Warm, sunny weather is a _____ for hanging clothes outdoors to dry.

2. The starfish had to _____ a leg after the eel grabbed it.

3. The punishment for a _____ crime is usually harsher than for an unplanned crime.

4. This problem will _____ if we don't come up with a solution now.

5. Jason helped Mr. Corelli _____ his old car; now it's as good as new.

6. Max asked Ashley to _____ what happened in the third act of the play.

7. Yolanda wears a helmet, knee pads, and elbow pads as a _____ when she goes rollerblading.

8. After six months apart, Anita and Stan had to _____ their lives.

9. The editor had to _____ news assignments before the holiday.

10. Volunteers will help _____ the Smiths' barn, which was destroyed by a fire.

Vocabulary Power

Lesson 18   Using Reading Skills
Learning from Context: Definitions

Have you ever wondered where certain words come from? Most dictionary entries include a brief note about the word's origin, or beginning. The note usually appears in square brackets, often toward the beginning of the entry. Several examples follow:

bovine (bō′vīn) *adj.* [from Latin *bov-, bos* ox, cow] **1.** of, relating to, or resembling bovines and especially the ox or cow **2.** having qualities (as placidity or dullness) characteristic of oxen or cows

czar (zär) *n.* [from Russian *tsar′,* from Latin *Caesar*] **1.** emperor, specifically the ruler of Russia until the 1917 revolution **2.** one having great power or authority

mecca (mek′ə) *n. often cap.* [*Mecca,* Saudi Arabia, a destination of pilgrims in the Islamic world] a center of activity sought as a goal by people sharing a common interest

mesmerize (mez′ mə rīz′, mes′-) *v.* [from Franz Mesmer, 1734–1815, an Austrian doctor who treated disease using a form of hypnotism] **1.** to subject to mesmerism, also to hypnotize **2.** spellbind

odyssey (od′ə sē) *n.* [from the *Odyssey,* the epic poem attributed to Homer recounting the long wanderings of Odysseus] **1.** a long wandering or voyage usually marked by many changes of fortune **2.** an intellectual or spiritual wandering or quest

EXERCISE

Use the sample entries above to answer each question about word origins.

1. Which word comes from the name of a Greek hero? What happened to this hero? _____

_____

_____

2. What is the Russian spelling of *czar?* From what older word and language does the Russian word come?

_____

_____

3. What is the origin of the word *mesmerize?* How does the meaning of this word relate to the word origin?

_____

_____

4. Which word comes from the name of a place? Describe this place. _____

_____

_____

5. How is a bovine person like a cow? _____

_____

_____

Vocabulary Power

Review: Unit 4

EXERCISE

Circle the word that best completes each sentence.

1. The landlord is planning to (relocate, recount, refurbish) several run-down apartment buildings on K Street.

2. Buyers at a flea market often try to (recount, haggle, gauge) with the sellers to get the best price.

3. The two countries had a(n) (obstruction, precondition, pact) to aid each other if an enemy invaded.

4. Fran decided on a(n) (novel, remote, invincible) costume for the party—she plans to come as a gas pump.

5. If you ask for a refund at that store, the owners will always (comply, imply, ford) with your request.

6. This chart will help to (illuminate, revive, reconstruct) the complex plan.

7. This chairperson had to (jut, reintegrate, imply) the members after the party lost the election.

8. The scientists' task is to (gauge, imply, revive) the amount of oxygen in the icy water near the South Pole.

9. Fran decided to take her dog on a(n) (rogue, frugal, invigorating) walk in the snow.

10. Building blocks are great—I can (reintegrate, reconstruct, ford) any building I have seen.

11. The lawyer argued that since the suspect had written his plan for the crime in a letter, the act was (invincible, premeditated, remote).

12. The other teams thought the Bulls were (invincible, novel, reckless) after three undefeated seasons.

13. Some animals can actually (recount, reintegrate, regenerate) their tails or digits if they lose them!

14. Please (refurbish, recount, revive) for us what you did on your vacation.

15. Darla always has money in her savings account because of her (frugal, novel, remote) shopping habits.

Vocabulary Power

Test: Unit 4

PART A

Circle the answer that best completes each sentence.

1. An example of a precaution is _____.
   - **a.** a car blocking a roadway
   - **b.** carrying extra batteries for a flashlight
   - **c.** an accident caused by carelessness
   - **d.** a toy that has many pieces

2. A rogue member of an organization is a _____.
   - **a.** follower
   - **b.** mischief-maker
   - **c.** pleasant person
   - **d.** lazy person

3. If you recount something, you _____.
   - **a.** perform a rescue
   - **b.** count backward
   - **c.** make a list
   - **d.** give a description

4. A precondition for moving on to the next grade level in school is _____.
   - **a.** passing the previous grade
   - **b.** taking part in sports
   - **c.** being admired by your teachers
   - **d.** having a large student body at your school

5. An example of a remote time in the past is _____.
   - **a.** yesterday
   - **b.** last year
   - **c.** the year 1950
   - **d.** the year 950

6. If you are dumbfounded, you are _____.
   - **a.** unintelligent
   - **b.** astonished
   - **c.** quiet
   - **d.** overjoyed

7. To revive a long-abandoned theater, people might _____.
   - **a.** begin to put on free plays there
   - **b.** turn it into an apartment building
   - **c.** do research to find out how old it was
   - **d.** change the location of the entrances

8. An obstruction is _____.
   - **a.** a formal agreement
   - **b.** something that blocks movement or progress
   - **c.** an argument against something
   - **d.** a building under construction

9. An example of a pact is a(n) _____.
   - **a.** decision of a committee to do a certain project
   - **b.** agreement with a friend to go to a certain movie
   - **c.** trade agreement between two countries
   - **d.** decision of two people to adopt a child

10. A vibrant person would be _____.
    - **a.** nervous
    - **b.** energetic
    - **c.** bored
    - **d.** tired

Vocabulary Power *continued*

PART B

Write the letter of the word that has the same meaning as the expression.

1. suggest or hint
    a. jut   **b.** imply   **c.** haggle   **d.** prefix

2. measurement of the thickness of sheet metal
    a. recurrence   **b.** reconstruction   **c.** gauge   **d.** obstruction

3. not dependably strong or solid
    a. unsound   **b.** invincible   **c.** vibrant   **d.** invigorating

4. build again
    a. refurbish   **b.** imply   **c.** revive   **d.** reconstruct

5. giving life and energy to
    a. gauging   **b.** invigorating   **c.** reintegrating   **d.** fording

6. restore to original strength
    a. illuminate   **b.** recur   **c.** regenerate   **d.** comply

7. stick out
    a. imply   **b.** ford   **c.** prefix   **d.** jut

8. bring back to life
    a. revive   **b.** recur   **c.** illuminate   **d.** imply

9. something that impedes
    a. precaution   **b.** pact   **c.** obstruction   **d.** precondition

10. happen again
    a. gauge   **b.** recur   **c.** haggle   **d.** imply

11. impossible to defeat
    a. novel   **b.** frugal   **c.** premeditated   **d.** invincible

12. clarify
    a. illuminate   **b.** recount   **c.** revive   **d.** reintegrate

13. negotiate over a price
    a. gauge   **b.** haggle   **c.** jut   **d.** revive

14. strikingly unusual
    a. vibrant   **b.** unsound   **c.** remote   **d.** novel

15. go along with another's wish or command
    a. gauge   **b.** refurbish   **c.** imply   **d.** comply

♪ Vocabulary Power

Lesson 19   Using Context Clues

Independence and self-reliance go hand in hand. You need to be able to stand on your own and trust your own abilities and judgment. You've probably experienced this. For example, as children grow into teenagers and take on more responsibilities, adults tend to give them more freedom. The words in this list relate to the idea of freedom.

Word List

chronicle	disheveled	indistinct	minimal
disclose	divert	intrigue	sibling
discord	independent		

EXERCISE A   Clues Matching

Each example below contains a clue about the meaning of the boldfaced word. Use the clue to guess the word's likely meaning. Write your guess above the word. Then, look up the word in a dictionary and write its meaning.

1. The **discord** between Democrats and Republicans is evident in their bitter debates.

   Dictionary definition _____

2. Grandfather clocks **intrigue** me; I'd like to learn more about how they are made.

   Dictionary definition _____

3. The reporter would not **disclose** the source of her information.

   Dictionary definition _____

4. **Independent** countries are sometimes forced to protect their freedom.

   Dictionary definition _____

5. His **disheveled** appearance—uncombed hair and unshaved face—showed that he had just awakened.

   Dictionary definition _____

6. My sister is my only **sibling;** I have no other sisters and no brothers.

   Dictionary definition _____

7. The police officers must **divert** traffic from the parade route.

   Dictionary definition _____

8. Without his glasses, John sees only **indistinct** figures on the movie screen.

   Dictionary definition _____

✣ | *Vocabulary Power* continued

9. This **chronicle** of immigration gives a day-by-day account of a Swedish family's journey to

    America in 1844.

    Dictionary definition _____

10. Because of her high blood pressure, Jodie uses a **minimal** amount of salt for seasoning.

    Dictionary definition _____

EXERCISE B Multiple-Meaning Words

Several of the vocabulary words have more than one meaning. Using your understanding of these meanings, write the vocabulary word that best describes each of the following people or situations.

1. the main clause of a sentence   _____

2. to record a newsworthy event as it happens   _____

3. a secret love affair between Jay and Lilly   _____

4. a person arguing with the boss   _____

5. basic requirements for presidency   _____

6. the skyline of a city enshrouded in fog   _____

7. a police officer rerouting traffic   _____

8. telling a secret to a friend   _____

9. a sister or brother   _____

10. your hair on a windy day   _____

EXERCISE C Sentence Completion

Circle the word that best completes each sentence.

1. My sister Jenny is my only (intrigue, sibling, chronicle).

2. The endings of those mystery stories always (disclose, divert, intrigue) me.

3. (Indistinct, Minimal, Independent) stores face strong competition today.

4. We can prevent congestion if we (divert, intrigue, disclose) traffic from the accident scene.

5. There was (intrigue, chronicle, discord) between the siblings over the toy.

6. We decided to (disclose, chronicle, divert) our trip across the country.

Vocabulary Power

Lesson 20   Using Synonyms

Freedom consists of two facets—freedom from negative aspects (such as poverty or repression) and freedom to do positive things (to move about freely, to express opinions in public, and to receive fair treatment under the law). Many of the words in this list relate to freedom.

Word List

agenda	bleak	priority	sullen
askew	eloquence	serenity	tempo
backlog	novice		

EXERCISE A Synonyms

Each boldfaced word below is paired with a synonym whose meaning you probably know. Think of other words related to the synonym and write them on the line provided. Then, look up the vocabulary word in a dictionary and write its meaning.

1. **backlog** : buildup _____

    Dictionary definition _____

2. **tempo** : rate _____

    Dictionary definition _____

3. **bleak** : gloomy _____

    Dictionary definition _____

4. **novice** : beginner _____

    Dictionary definition _____

5. **eloquence** : persuasiveness _____

    Dictionary definition _____

EXERCISE B Clues Matching

Use the clues below to guess each boldfaced word's likely meaning. Write your guess above the word; then, look up the word in a dictionary and write its meaning.

1. After a mild earthquake shook the house, the pictures on the wall were **askew.**

    Dictionary definition _____

2. Kareem distributed the **agenda** to be covered in the meeting.

    Dictionary definition _____

Vocabulary Power *continued*

3. Still angry with her sister, Gina wore a **sullen** expression and said nothing during dinner.

Dictionary definition _____

4. Mr. Thorndike enjoyed the shady **serenity** of his backyard.

Dictionary definition _____

5. Replacing the broken windows is a **priority,** but we must also repaint all the rooms.

Dictionary definition _____

EXERCISE C **Word Association**
Write the vocabulary word that best fits each example.

1. quality of a persuasive speech   _____

2. buildup of orders that need to be filled   _____

3. list of tasks a club wants to accomplish   _____

4. rate of speed of a piece of music   _____

5. most important goal to achieve   _____

6. a silent and moody person   _____

7. a future without hope   _____

8. an inner feeling of peace and calm   _____

9. a cap sitting lopsided on your head   _____

10. a beginning skateboarder   _____

Vocabulary Power

Lesson 21   Latin Word Roots

Many English words have roots that come from Latin, the language spoken by the Romans. For example, the words *vocal* and *revoke* share the Latin root *voc,* which means "call" or "voice." Recognizing Latin roots can often help you figure out the meanings of unfamiliar words.

Word List

attain	endurance	infraction	specimen
consecutive	execute	retain	spectacle
duration	fragment		

EXERCISE A   Word Roots

Write two words from the list that share each root. After each word, write its dictionary definition.

dur (hard, lasting)

1. _____

2. _____

frag, fract (break)

3. _____

4. _____

secut (follow)

5. _____

6. _____

spec (look)

7. _____

8. _____

tain (hold)

9. _____

10. _____

Vocabulary Power *continued*

EXERCISE B Usage

Draw a line through the italicized expression and, above it, write the vocabulary word that fits.

1. Marlene picked up a *piece* of the broken vase that the cat had knocked over.

2. For this twenty-five-mile race, runners must have *the ability to hold up under stress.*

3. Repeating or using new information can help you *keep* it in your memory.

4. Lamont, a skilled diver and swimmer, will now *carry out* a swan dive from the high board.

5. The *period of existence* of the Roman Empire was about five hundred years.

6. Brad hopes to *reach* the rank of Eagle Scout by the age of sixteen.

7. Compared with most oak trees, this *example* is not very healthy.

8. The soccer player caught the referee's attention with his *violation of the rules*—deliberately tripping an opposing player.

EXERCISE C Questions and Answers

Answer *yes* or *no* to each question. Explain your answer, using your understanding of the boldfaced word.

1. If a president of the United States cannot serve for more than two **consecutive** terms of four years each, may he serve for twelve years?

   _____

   _____

2. Is a fireworks display an example of a **spectacle**?

   _____

   _____

3. Could you understand an entire conversation if you heard only a **fragment** of it?

   _____

   _____

4. When you go to another state, do you **retain** your rights as a U.S. citizen?

   _____

   _____

Vocabulary Power

Lesson 22   Suffixes That Form Adjectives

A suffix is a word ending that can be added to a word or root. Adding a suffix to a word or root may change its meaning. Words ending in the suffixes listed below are always adjectives.

Suffix	Meaning	Example
-able, -ible	able or capable of	terrible (terror + ible)
-ent	performing/causing a specific action	absorbent (absorb + ent)
-ive	tending to	creative (create + ive)
-ous, -ious	full of; possessing	joyous (joy + ous)
-y	have the character of; like; showing	slimy (slime + y)

Word List

affluent	comprehensible	fortuitous	imperative
arbitrary	deceptive	haughty	luscious
capable	diligent		

EXERCISE A   Suffixes

Write two adjectives from the list for each suffix below; then, write the dictionary definition.

y

1. _____

2. _____

-ent

3. _____

4. _____

-able, -ible

5. _____

6. _____

-ous, -ious

7. _____

8. _____

Vocabulary Power *continued*

-ive

9. _____

10. _____

EXERCISE B **Word Association**
Write the vocabulary word that could describe each example.

1. a necessary duty   _____

2. arrests based on type of car   _____

3. a lucky break   _____

4. an upscale neighborhood   _____

5. a counterfeit bill   _____

6. a chocolate candy that melts in your mouth   _____

7. someone who looks down his nose at you   _____

8. instructions that are easy to follow   _____

EXERCISE C **Synonyms**
Write the vocabulary word that is a synonym for each word below.

1. accidental   _____

2. delicious   _____

3. skilled   _____

4. understandable   _____

5. misleading   _____

6. industrious   _____

7. arrogant   _____

8. wealthy   _____

Vocabulary Power

Lesson 23   Using Reading Skills
Learning from Context: Examples
When you encounter a new word in your reading, you can often use the context, or the surrounding words, to help figure out the word's meaning. Sometimes the sentence includes examples that give you hints about the meaning of the word, as in the following sentence:

> The senator delivered a tirade on the new health-care bill; he shouted and pounded his fists on the podium, denouncing the wording.

From the example, you can figure out that a *tirade* is a long, angry speech.

EXERCISE A

In each sentence, circle the examples that help you understand the meaning of the boldfaced term. Then, write a possible definition of the word.

1. At the public hearing, several people gave **testimony** before the city council members. Ms. Mazoud

   said the new store would create too much traffic, while Mr. Nelson said it would create additional jobs.

   Testimony probably means _____

2. The chest was full of bangles, inexpensive bead necklaces, and other **trinkets.**

   Trinkets probably means _____

3. Bears are **omnivorous:** they eat plants, such as berries; insects, such as ants and grubs; and also meat.

   Omnivorous probably means _____

4. Sam is a **laconic** person. When I asked if he were going to the concert, he answered just, "Nope."

   When I asked why, he just shrugged his shoulders.

   Laconic probably means _____

EXERCISE B

Look up each boldfaced word in a dictionary and write its definition. Then, before each word, rate the accuracy of your definition from Exercise A on a scale of 1 to 5, with 5 being most accurate.

_____ 1. testimony _____

_____ 2. trinket _____

_____ 3. omnivorous _____

_____ 4. laconic _____

Vocabulary Power

Review: Unit 5

EXERCISE

Circle the word that best completes each sentence.

1. On one (fragment, specimen, agenda) of the torn-up note, Irene could read the words "Love, Joel."

2. After the crushing defeat, the football team was in a (haughty, bleak, diligent) mood.

3. Miguel grew up in poverty, but today he has his own business and a(n) (affluent, independent, luscious) lifestyle.

4. I haven't seen the movie yet, so please don't (divert, disclose, execute) the ending.

5. It was a (fortuitous, comprehensible, deceptive) moment for us when we got tickets to the sold-out concert.

6. Jamie is my older sister; my younger (spectacle, novice, sibling) is Jessica.

7. In the distance, they spotted two (independent, indistinct, consecutive) figures coming up the hill.

8. Of my three goals for the summer, learning to swim is my (fragment, priority, backlog).

9. The parade was a (tempo, spectacle, chronicle), featuring over a hundred brightly decorated floats and twelve of the best brass bands in the country.

10. Because of her (disheveled, imperative, arbitrary) appearance at the interview, she did not get the job.

11. Stephen was given detention for his serious (imperative, eloquence, infraction).

12. A huge (tempo, backlog, chronicle) of orders had to be filled.

13. Fourteen (consecutive, comprehensible, sullen) days of rain have created flooding problems.

14. In order to get the job, Jan had to show he was (capable, independent, haughty) of handling it.

15. It is (comprehensible, imperative, fortuitous) that I speak to the general immediately!

Vocabulary Power

Test: Unit 5

PART A

Circle the vocabulary word that you would most likely use in writing about each boldfaced topic.

1. **history** : chronicle, duration, tempo

2. **music** : backlog, imperative, tempo

3. **laws** : discord, endurance, infraction

4. **meetings** : agenda, spectacle, novice

5. **speaking** : specimen, eloquence, sibling

PART B

Circle the letter of the word that best completes the sentence.

1. The garden contains many beautiful tea roses, but this _____ is especially lovely.
   a. sibling   **b.** agenda   **c.** fragment   **d.** specimen

2. *Science for Dummies* features a(n) _____ article on cloning.
   a. comprehensible **b.** indistinct   **c.** consecutive   **d.** independent

3. Sled dogs have amazing _____; they can pull a loaded sled for hours.
   a. serenity   **b.** duration   **c.** endurance   **d.** discord

4. Judy managed to _____ her sense of humor despite losing her bid for the job.
   a. attain   **b.** disclose   **c.** divert   **d.** retain

5. Karen was sick for four _____ days, Saturday through Tuesday.
   a. consecutive **b.** minimal   **c.** imperative   **d.** arbitrary

6. The banner hung _____, because the beam was crooked.
   a. arbitrary   **b.** indistinct   **c.** luscious   **d.** askew

7. The satisfying dinner included a(n) _____ selection of desserts.
   a. deceptive   **b.** luscious   **c.** sullen   **d.** indistinct

8. The librarians worked overtime to check in the _____ of returns.
   a. duration   **b.** discord   **c.** backlog   **d.** specimen

9. The _____ weather forecast caused the picnic to be canceled.
   a. fortuitous   **b.** bleak   **c.** capable   **d.** haughty

10. Locating clean water was their top _____ on the deserted island.
    a. priority   **b.** intrigue   **c.** imperative   **d.** testimony

⁊ Vocabulary Power *continued*

PART C

Circle the letter of the word that has the same meaning as the boldfaced expression.

1. reach a goal
   a. intrigue   **b.** attain   **c.** retain   **d.** chronicle

2. small
   a. diligent   **b.** minimal   **c.** consecutive   **d.** imperative

3. accidental
   a. capable   **b.** disheveled   **c.** arbitrary   **d.** fortuitous

4. beginner
   a. specimen   **b.** novice   **c.** tempo   **d.** imperative

5. a brother or sister
   a. fragment   **b.** agenda   **c.** sibling   **d.** priority

6. state of complete calm
   a. serenity   **b.** discord   **c.** eloquence   **d.** spectacle

7. period during which something lasts
   a. endurance   **b.** infraction   **c.** agenda   **d.** duration

8. untidy
   a. indistinct   **b.** diligent   **c.** disheveled   **d.** deceptive

9. reveal
   a. divert   **b.** retain   **c.** intrigue   **d.** disclose

10. not sharply outlined
   a. sullen   **b.** indistinct   **c.** imperative   **d.** independent

PART D

Circle the word that means most nearly the opposite of the boldfaced word.

1. **honest** : haughty, deceptive, bleak

2. **poor** : arbitrary, affluent, luscious

3. **cheerful** : sullen, minimal, capable

4. **expert** : specimen, chronicle, novice

5. **careless** : diligent, consecutive, indistinct

Vocabulary Power

Lesson 24   Using Synonyms

Have you ever found yourself thinking, "Aha!" "That's it!" or "How true!"? These exclamations mark moments of insight. Such moments come when you see deeply into a situation or grasp a valuable truth about life. The words in this list can help you think, speak, and write about insights.

Word List

crouch	envision	lurk	surpass
diverse	incompatible	superb	valiant
envelop	jog		

EXERCISE A **Synonyms**

Each boldfaced word below is paired with a synonym whose meaning you probably know. Think of other words related to the synonym and write them on the line provided. Then, look up the word in a dictionary and write its meaning.

1. **surpass** : excel _____

   Dictionary definition _____

2. **envelop** : surround _____

   Dictionary definition _____

3. **jog** : nudge _____

   Dictionary definition _____

4. **envision** : imagine _____

   Dictionary definition _____

5. **diverse** : different _____

   Dictionary definition _____

6. **crouch** : cringe _____

   Dictionary definition _____

7. **incompatible** : conflicting _____

   Dictionary definition _____

8. **superb** : excellent _____

   Dictionary definition _____

Vocabulary Power *continued*

9. **valiant** : brave _____

Dictionary definition _____

10. **lurk** : wait _____

Dictionary definition _____

EXERCISE B   Usage
Use the meaning of the boldfaced word to answer each question.

1. In what way is the population of your town or city **diverse**?

_____

2. If a piece of furniture were of **superb** quality, what would it be like?

_____

3. Describe two foods that you think are **incompatible**.

_____

4. What is an example of a **valiant** act?

_____

5. What are some jungle animals that **lurk,** waiting for their prey?

_____

EXERCISE C   Context Clues
Write the vocabulary word that fits each clue.

1. Fog could do this to a house.   _____

2. A come-from-behind racer could do this to the front runner.   _____

3. A hungry bear might do this at a campground.   _____

4. A photograph could do this to your memory of an event.   _____

5. A hunter might do this in tall grass to stay hidden.   _____

6. People often do this about the future.   _____

7. A hero is often considered this.   _____

8. Two people who don't get along are considered this.   _____

9. A wonderful tasting food could be called this.   _____

10. A zoo with animals from around the world has this type of collection.   _____

Vocabulary Power

Lesson 25   Words from Technology

The English language is ever changing. New words are added every year. Some of these words come from new or expanding fields of technology. Computer technology has brought many new words into the language. The ten words below can help you use and describe computer technology.

Word List

byte	format	multimedia	save
delete	microprocessor	peripheral	zoom
disk	monitor		

EXERCISE A **Computer Definitions**

Look up each word in a dictionary and write the meaning that is related to computers.

1. save _____

2. delete _____

3. format _____

4. disk _____

5. zoom _____

6. multimedia _____

7. microprocessor _____

8. monitor _____

9. peripheral _____

10. byte _____

EXERCISE B **Clues Matching**

Write the vocabulary word that matches each clue.

1. This is often considered the brain of a calculator or computer. _____

2. This kind of device must be hooked up to the computer to be useful. _____

3. You could store a list of names and addresses on this. _____

4. A table with columns and rows is an example of this. _____

5. This is the amount of memory needed to store a tiny piece of information. _____

Vocabulary Power *continued*

6. An encyclopedia on computer that includes pictures and

   musical recordings is an example of this.   _____

7. In a group photograph, you would do this to view one person's face close up.   _____

8. To shorten a sentence, you would do this to several words in the sentence.   _____

9. If you write a letter on a computer and want to edit it later, you would do this to the letter. _____

10. This device has a viewing screen similar to a television.   _____

EXERCISE C Usage
Answer each question using your understanding of the boldfaced word.

1. What is the **format** of this section? _____

   What change could you make in this format if you were redesigning the page? _____

   _____

2. Is a **microprocessor** an example of a **peripheral?** Explain.

   _____

   _____

3. Describe what a **multimedia** computer program called *Animals of Africa* might be like to use.

   _____

   _____

4. If you **save** a document in a program, what are you doing?

   _____

   _____

5. Why might you **delete** a document on a **disk?**

   _____

   _____

Vocabulary Power

Lesson 26 Using Synonyms and Antonyms

The English language is full of synonyms. A synonym is a word that has a similar meaning to another word. For example, the words *hearty, well,* and *hardy* are all synonyms for *healthy.* Knowing synonyms for words can help you choose the word that expresses a fact or thought exactly. For example, you might choose to say "*elderly* woman" rather than "*old* woman" if you want to show a respectful attitude.

Knowing antonyms for words is also helpful. An *antonym* is a word that means the opposite, or nearly the opposite, of another word. For example, *ill, unhealthy,* and *ailing* are all antonyms for *healthy.*

Word List			
detached	imperceptible	meticulous	prevalent
hospitable	initial	pliant	temporary
humid	juvenile		

EXERCISE A Synonyms

Each boldfaced word below is paired with a synonym whose meaning you probably know. Think of other words related to the synonym and write them on the line provided. Then, look up the vocabulary word in a dictionary and write its meaning.

1. **juvenile** : childish _____

   Dictionary definition _____

2. **temporary** : brief _____

   Dictionary definition _____

3. **meticulous** : finicky _____

   Dictionary definition _____

4. **detached** : distant _____

   Dictionary definition _____

5. **hospitable** : kind _____

   Dictionary definition _____

6. **imperceptible** : invisible _____

   Dictionary definition _____

7. **pliant** : flexible _____

   Dictionary definition _____

Vocabulary Power *continued*

8. humid : muggy _____

Dictionary definition _____

9. initial : beginning _____

Dictionary definition _____

10. prevalent : widespread _____

Dictionary definition _____

EXERCISE B Antonyms

Knowing the antonym, or word most opposite in meaning, of a word strengthens your understanding of the word's meaning. Write an antonym for each vocabulary word below.

1. initial _____

2. pliant _____

3. meticulous _____

4. prevalent _____

5. juvenile _____

6. humid _____

7. detached _____

8. temporary _____

9. imperceptible _____

10. hospitable _____

EXERCISE C Sentence Completion

Complete each sentence with the correct vocabulary word.

1. We stayed with a(n) _____ family in Guatemala, who welcomed us warmly and made us feel at home.

2. The _____ plastic fence was set up in November to help keep snow from blowing onto the road.

3. During the movie, making noises, throwing popcorn, and other _____ behavior will not be tolerated!

4. After soaking in hot water for several hours, the thin strips of wood became _____ and could be woven together.

5. Furniture experts could tell that one of the chairs was antique and the other one new, but to the average person the differences were _____.

6. My _____ impression of her was positive, but later I changed my mind.

Vocabulary Power

Lesson 27   Number Prefixes

A prefix is a word part added at the beginning of a word or root. Some prefixes stand for a number, such as *tri-*, which means "three." The prefix changes the root's meaning. For example, the word *trimonthly (tri + monthly)* means "occurring every three months." Six number prefixes, along with meanings and examples, are listed in the chart below.

Prefix	Meaning	Example	Definition
semi-	half	semilunar	shaped like a half moon
uni-	one	unicycle	cycle with one wheel
bi-	two	bicep	a muscle with two points of origin
quadri-	four	quadruped	a four-footed animal
penta-	five	pentagon	a five-sided figure
milli-	thousandth	milliliter	one thousandth of a liter

Word List

biped	millisecond	semiannual	unidirectional
bisect	pentathlon	semicircle	unify
millennium	quadruple		

EXERCISE A Prefixes

Write the words from the list that share the same prefix. Then, look up the meaning of each word in a dictionary and write its definition.

uni- (one)

1. _____

2. _____

penta- (five)

3. _____

   _____

quadri- (four)

4. _____

milli- (thousand)

5. _____

6. _____

♒ Vocabulary Power continued

semi- (half)

7. _____

8. _____

bi- (two)

9. _____

10. _____

EXERCISE B **Usage**

If the boldfaced word is used correctly in the sentence, write *correct* above it. If not, draw a line through it and write the correct vocabulary word above it.

1. The solstice, a day with equal hours of night and day, is a **unidirectional** event, occurring in the fall and in the spring.

2. The year 2000 has been celebrated as the start of a new **millisecond**.

3. If they **bisect** the size of their cattle herd, which now contains one hundred cattle, they will have a herd of four hundred.

4. Mario's strongest events in the **millennium** are the sprinting, hurdling, and long jumping, but he is weaker at throwing the discus and the javelin.

5. This **unidirectional** microphone will pick up the speaker's voice but not other sounds from around the room.

EXERCISE C **Context Clues**

Write the word that could describe each example.

1. a human being   _____

2. arrangement of children to listen to a story read aloud   _____

3. cut a pizza into two halves   _____

4. combine two groups into one   _____

5. time that is much faster than the blink of an eye _____

EXERCISE D **Word Web**

Another meaning of the prefix *semi-* is "partial." For example, *semisecret* information is not publicly announced but widely known. On a separate sheet of paper, work with a partner to create a web of words with the prefix *semi-*. Take turns giving or looking up the meaning of each word.

Vocabulary Power

Vocabulary Power

Lesson 28   Using Reading Skills
Using a Dictionary: Multiple-Meaning Words

As you've probably noticed, many words have more than one meaning. In a dictionary entry for a word, these meanings are listed by number. Usually, the meanings are listed from most common to least common or from general to specific, as in the entry below.

> **marshal** (mär′shəl) *n.* **1.** a military officer of the highest rank in some countries **2.** a U.S. government officer who carries out court orders and has duties similar to those of a sheriff **3.** the head of a fire department **4.** the person in charge of a parade *v.* **1.** to arrange or place troops in line for a parade or battle **2.** to arrange, place, or set in order **3.** to enlist and organize **4.** to lead ceremoniously; to usher

EXERCISE

The word *marshal* appears in each sentence below. Write the part of speech (noun or verb) and the number of the specific definition that fits the meaning of the word as it is used in the sentence.

1. Before we can make a decision, we need to **marshal** all the facts. _____

2. The **marshal** of the Memorial Day parade waved to the crowd from

   the back of a streamlined white convertible. _____

3. Colonel Rosencranz will **marshal** his troops on the ridge to wait

   for the enemy attack. _____

4. General Ferdinand Foch was the **marshal** of the French, English,

   and American armies in World War I. _____

5. The fire **marshal** will speak at a schoolwide assembly this week

   on the topic of fire safety. _____

6. The president ordered a U.S. **marshal** to carry out the

   desegregation order of the federal court. _____

7. Volunteers are talking to people at grocery stores to try to

   marshal support for improving the city's parks. _____

8. Each teacher should **marshal** her students down the steps to the gym. _____

Vocabulary Power

Review: Unit 6

EXERCISE A

Circle the word that best completes each sentence.

1. The change in the position of the sculpture was (imperceptible, unidirectional, incompatible) to most museum visitors.

2. The guidance counselor encouraged Lena to try to (envision, envelop, unify) a successful future for herself.

3. To improve the overall performance of his computer, Ron is thinking of replacing the (millennium, multimedia, microprocessor) with a better one.

4. The community center holds (prevalent, semiannual, quadruple) potluck suppers in January and June for everyone in the neighborhood.

5. Don't (zoom, lurk, jog) behind that curtain; come out and show yourself!

6. Harvey keeps (diverse, meticulous, temporary) records of every penny he saves or spends.

7. To get through the low passage in the cave, we had to (crouch, unify, delete) as we walked.

8. The information was easy to read because it was presented in the (monitor, byte, format) of a list.

9. The ambassador attempted to (delete, unify, surpass) the two sides at the bargaining table.

10. The producers of television commercials expect children to be (incompatible, juvenile, pliant).

EXERCISE B

Circle the vocabulary word that you would be most likely to use in writing about each boldfaced topic.

1. **time** : millisecond, disk, meticulous

2. **sports** : semicircle, byte, pentathlon

3. **computers** : diverse, pentathlon, disk

4. **weather** : envision, humid, microprocessor

5. **children** : juvenile, unify, lurk

6. **animals** : surpass, multimedia, biped

Vocabulary Power

Test: Unit 6

PART A

Circle the answer that best completes each sentence.

1. An example of something that is pliant is _____.
   - **a.** a wooden board
   - **b.** a mirror
   - **c.** a snow shovel
   - **d.** a garden hose

2. A prevalent style of clothing is _____.
   - **a.** a style worn by most people
   - **b.** a style worn by a few people
   - **c.** a style that is attractive
   - **d.** a style that is unattractive

3. An example of something that could commonly envelop an industrial city is _____.
   - **a.** a rainbow
   - **b.** a plague of locusts
   - **c.** smog
   - **d.** a blanket of air freshener

4. An example of a temporary shelter is _____.
   - **a.** an apartment building
   - **b.** a log cabin
   - **c.** a tent
   - **d.** a doghouse

5. If you quadruple the number 4, the result is _____.
   - **a.** 32
   - **b.** 16
   - **c.** 8
   - **d.** 1

6. A semicircle looks most like _____.
   - **a.** the letter O
   - **b.** the letter C
   - **c.** the number 8
   - **d.** the letter I

7. An example of a biped is _____.
   - **a.** a horse
   - **b.** a worm
   - **c.** a bee
   - **d.** a man

8. The function of a monitor is to _____.
   - **a.** display words and images
   - **b.** operate the computer
   - **c.** store information
   - **d.** send messages over telephone lines

9. If you rated a meal as superb, you thought the meal was _____.
   - **a.** average
   - **b.** terrible
   - **c.** excellent
   - **d.** unfilling

10. An example of something that might fill a byte of computer memory is _____.
    - **a.** a letter of the alphabet
    - **b.** a chapter of a book
    - **c.** an encyclopedia
    - **d.** a long list of companies

Vocabulary Power *continued*

Choose the letter of the word that has nearly the same meaning as the word or phrase.

1. combined use of several forms of communication
   - **a.** discourage
   - **b.** pentathlon
   - **c.** multimedia
   - **d.** millennium

2. go beyond
   - **a.** surpass
   - **b.** unify
   - **c.** quadruple
   - **d.** zoom

3. machine or device that works in combination with a computer
   - **a.** microprocessor
   - **b.** byte
   - **c.** millisecond
   - **d.** peripheral

4. cut or divide into two parts
   - **a.** envision
   - **b.** bisect
   - **c.** envelop
   - **d.** lurk

5. differing from one another
   - **a.** meticulous
   - **b.** pliant
   - **c.** valiant
   - **d.** diverse

6. unconnected
   - **a.** prevalent
   - **b.** detached
   - **c.** semiannual
   - **d.** humid

7. inclined to treat guests kindly
   - **a.** hospitable
   - **b.** initial
   - **c.** superb
   - **d.** pliant

8. period of one thousand years
   - **a.** pentathlon
   - **b.** semicircle
   - **c.** millennium
   - **d.** millisecond

9. remove or erase
   - **a.** jog
   - **b.** surpass
   - **c.** save
   - **d.** delete

10. first
    - **a.** unidirectional
    - **b.** initial
    - **c.** envelop
    - **d.** bisect

Vocabulary Power

Lesson 29   Using Synonyms

The English word *dignity* comes from a word used by the ancient Romans, *dignus,* meaning "worthy." People who have dignity are worthy, or admirable, because they possess an inner strength and strong self-respect. The words in this list relate to the idea of dignity.

Word List

abide	conspicuous	ponder	universal
ban	humane	token	virtue
catastrophe	merge		

EXERCISE A   Synonyms

Each boldfaced vocabulary word below is paired with a synonym whose meaning you probably know. Think of other related words and write them on the line provided. Then, look up the vocabulary word in a dictionary and write its meaning.

1. **humane** : merciful _____

   Dictionary definition _____

2. **abide** : await _____

   Dictionary definition _____

3. **universal** : general _____

   Dictionary definition _____

4. **merge** : combine _____

   Dictionary definition _____

5. **ban** : forbid _____

   Dictionary definition _____

6. **conspicuous** : noticeable _____

   Dictionary definition _____

7. **ponder** : consider _____

   Dictionary definition _____

8. **token** : symbol _____

   Dictionary definition _____

🎵 *Vocabulary Power* continued

9. catastrophe : disaster _____

Dictionary definition _____

10. virtue : goodness _____

Dictionary definition _____

EXERCISE B Usage

If the boldfaced word is used correctly in the sentence, write *correct* above it. If not, draw a line through it and write the correct word above it.

1. Toys Unlimited and Toyco, Inc., plan to **abide** into one company.

2. Do you know why they **ban** glass bottles at sporting events?

3. Please accept these flowers as a **virtue** of my thanks for all your work.

4. The desire for respect is **universal** among human beings.

5. I just cannot **ponder** a dirty house when relatives are coming.

6. Jason was **humane** in the team photo because he alone was out of uniform.

EXERCISE C Questions and Answers

Answer each question with a *yes* or *no*. Use the meaning of the boldfaced word to explain your answer.

1. Is hitting your finger with a hammer a **catastrophe**?

_____

2. In your opinion, is being patient a **virtue**?

_____

3. Is the **Humane** Society a good name for a group that accepts lost or mistreated animals?

_____

4. Do you **ponder** your choice of clothes each day?

_____

Vocabulary Power

Lesson 30   Suffixes That Form Verbs

A suffix is a word ending that can be added to a word or root. Some suffixes, such as *-ize, -ify,* and *-ate* tell you that the word is a verb. The suffix *-ize* means "to become like" or "to treat with." The suffixes *-ate* and *-fy* mean "to make" or "to cause to become."

Word List

customize	facilitate	indicate	mediate
electrify	fortify	integrate	socialize
fabricate	glorify		

EXERCISE A **Multiple-Meaning Words**

Some of the vocabulary words have more than one meaning. Use context clues to determine which meaning of the boldfaced word is being used. Then, write the dictionary definition that applies.

1. Saphron had to **indicate** her desire to join the committee.

_____

2. I just knew he would **fabricate** an excuse!

_____

3. *My Fair Lady* tells the tale of a professor who decides to **socialize** a poor working woman.

_____

4. Ambassadors frequently have to **mediate** disputes between countries.

_____

5. Gerry decided to **customize** his new car with a unique paint job.

_____

6. We need to **fortify** our house against the incoming hurricane.

_____

7. Schools were required to **integrate** in the 1960s.

_____

Vocabulary Power *continued*

8. The elaborate dresses and stunning bouquets seemed to **glorify** the banquet hall.

_____

9. The coach knew that a touchdown was needed to **electrify** the crowd.

_____

10. An attentive puppy will **facilitate** her recovery from her illness.

_____

EXERCISE B Usage

If the boldfaced word is used correctly in the sentence, write *correct* above it. If not, draw a line through it and write the correct vocabulary word above it.

1. Rochelle is part of a team of volunteers who help **integrate** serious disagreements between other students.

2. In this part of the car factory, the workers **fabricate** hoods, corner panels, and bumpers.

3. These dials on the control panel of the airplane **mediate** altitude, air pressure, and speed.

4. After we conduct the survey, we will **indicate** the results with the information we already have.

5. The acrobats' amazing final trick is guaranteed to **fortify** the audience.

EXERCISE C Word Association

Write the vocabulary word that matches each example.

1. design a kitchen so a person in a wheelchair can use it easily _____

2. add extra stones to make the wall of a castle thicker _____

3. go out to movies and parties with other people _____

4. praise someone as one of the greatest people who ever lived _____

5. make the adjustment of recent immigrants to a new country easier _____

Name _____ Date _____ Class _____

Vocabulary Power

Lesson 31   Compound Words

Some words are a combination of two or more other words. *Northwest, wild rice,* and *know-it-all* are all compound words. Notice that a compound word may be spelled "closed up," with a hyphen joining the words, or with a space between the words.

> **Word List**
>
> | | | | |
> |---|---|---|---|
> | cross-reference | overhang | self-conscious | underscore |
> | cross section | overhaul | single-minded | undertake |
> | high-minded | self-assured | | |

EXERCISE A   Compound Words

Analyze the words in each compound word to match it with the correct definition.

1. reference from one part of a book, index, or file to another part containing related information _____

2. take upon oneself; decide to do _____

3. having one driving purpose or goal _____

4. having or showing confidence _____

5. projecting over the edge of a building _____

6. a cut straight through the middle of something to reveal its contents _____

7. having high ideals; noble _____

8. renovate thoroughly _____

9. aware of oneself; especially, uncomfortably self-aware _____

10. to emphasize, such as underlining _____

EXERCISE B   Clues Matching

Write the word that matches the clue.

1. If you did this to an old motor scooter, it could run like new. _____

2. You could do this with a new sport. _____

3. You can see the rings of a tree in this. _____

4. If you believed in volunteering your time, you might be called this. _____

5. Part of a tall building to which Christmas lights and banners are attached. _____

6. A person who neglects everything else for one goal is this. _____

Vocabulary Power *continued*

7. "See page 23" is an example. _____

8. You could do this by drawing a line under an important word. _____

9. You might feel this way if someone made fun of your hairstyle. _____

10. Someone who is at ease with many kinds of people is this. _____

EXERCISE C **Usage**

Answer each question using your understanding of the vocabulary word.

1. Why might a person **undertake** a difficult task?

_____

2. In giving a speech, what could you do to **underscore** the main idea?

_____

3. Describe a **cross section** of an orange.

_____

4. Give an example of a **cross-reference** you might see in a textbook.

_____

5. Why might someone be **single-minded** about a goal?

_____

6. What is something a **self-assured** person might say?

_____

7. Name three places you could find an **overhang**.

_____

8. What qualities might a **high-minded** person have?

_____

9. Other than a car, what machines could be improved by an **overhaul**?

_____

10. What is something that might make a person feel **self-conscious?**

_____

Vocabulary Power

Lesson 32   Using Reading Skills
Learning from Context: Comparison and Contrast

When you encounter a new word in your reading, you can often use context clues, or clues in the surrounding text, to figure out the word's meaning. Sometimes you can compare or contrast the word with more familiar words that have similar or opposite meanings. Certain words, such as *like, also,* and *too,* can signal a comparison. Other words, such as *but, unlike,* and *however,* can signal a contrast.

Comparison
The new owner plans to demolish the bookstore and tear down the bakery next to it *too*.
<u>Explanation</u>: The word *too* signals a comparison: the bookstore and bakery are being treated alike, so you can guess that *demolish* means "tear down."

Contrast
That remark is *not* a compliment; it's an affront.
<u>Explanation</u>: The word *not* signals a contrast between the word *compliment* and the word *affront.* So you can guess that *affront* means "insult."

EXERCISE

In each sentence, circle the word that signals a comparison or contrast. Then, write the meaning of the boldfaced word based on the context clues.

1. Cassie drew a **valid** conclusion from the evidence, but Raymond's conclusion was incorrect.

    _____

2. The hundred-year-old oak tree in front of the school is still **vigorous;** the younger maples are

    also flourishing.

    _____

3. Conchita's response to the first question was **vague;** however, she answered the second question

    very clearly.

    _____

4. Like the downtown areas in many small towns that have **vacant** shops, our downtown also has

    several empty stores on Main Street.

    _____

5. In contrast to the **vast** lawns found in Richwood, the yards in this neighborhood are tiny.

    _____

6. Emperor Ming of the planet Mondo is a **vindictive** character, and his son, the prince, is equally vengeful.

    _____

Vocabulary Power

Review: Unit 7

EXERCISE A

Circle the letter of the word that could describe each example.

1. putting others' needs ahead of your own
   a. ban **b.** virtue **c.** underscore **d.** catastrophe

2. a law that applies to all members of a society
   a. conspicuous **b.** single-minded **c.** universal **d.** high-minded

3. a civil war that leaves a country in ruins
   a. catastrophe **b.** token **c.** cross section **d.** overhang

4. a card sent to someone as a sign of affection
   a. token **b.** virtue **c.** cross-reference **d.** universal

5. entry in a book's index telling you where to find more information on a topic
   a. underscore **b.** ban **c.** token **d.** cross-reference

6. how a red bandage would look on your nose
   a. self-assured **b.** overhang **c.** conspicuous **d.** high-minded

7. Red Cross workers who comfort and help suffering people
   a. universal **b.** humane **c.** self-conscious **d.** single-minded

8. thin slice from the middle of an object that allows you to see its internal parts under a microscope
   a. overhang **b.** catastrophe **c.** ban **d.** cross section

EXERCISE B

Circle the word in parentheses that best completes each sentence.

1. Marcus always has a positive attitude; I wish I were as (self-assured, self-conscious, humane) as he is.

2. The grand finale of the fireworks display never fails to (fortify, underscore, electrify) the crowd.

3. Hank used pieces of plywood he found in a dumpster to (integrate, fabricate, overhaul) a playhouse for his little brother.

4. Do you believe that smiles always (ponder, indicate, ban) happiness?

5. Does the park (ban, merge, customize) dune buggies on this beach?

6. Many people take time to (mediate, socialize, overhang) on weekends.

7. Anita decided to (overhaul, integrate, undertake) the monumental task of entertaining the six-year-olds.

Vocabulary Power

Test: Unit 7

PART A

Circle the letter of the correct definition for each boldfaced word.

1. single-minded
   a. having one brain
   b. having great confidence
   c. have one driving goal
   d. having high ideals

2. merge
   a. melt
   b. mumble
   c. combine
   d. complain

3. ponder
   a. think about carefully
   b. show kindness
   c. settle differences
   d. walk without purpose

4. underscore
   a. estimate
   b. repair
   c. attempt
   d. emphasize

5. integrate
   a. repeat a message
   b. serve as a sign of something else
   c. unite with something else
   d. make easy or easier

6. customize
   a. make into a customer
   b. change to suit personal desires
   c. adopt a new custom
   d. give high praise to

7. facilitate
   a. make easier
   b. see through
   c. make up
   d. breathe into

8. undertake
   a. speed past
   b. prepare for death
   c. decide to attempt
   d. travel beneath

9. overhang
   a. make too large
   b. sit behind
   c. protrude over the edge
   d. pester someone constantly

10. abide
    a. develop affection for
    b. weigh in the mind
    c. prohibit by official order
    d. wait patiently for

Vocabulary Power *continued*

PART B

Circle the letter of the expression that best completes each sentence.

1. An example of something you might mediate is _____.
   - **a.** the meaning of a religious belief
   - **b.** a conflict between two people
   - **c.** a baseball game
   - **d.** a cheeseburger

2. A high-minded person has _____.
   - **a.** noble ideals
   - **b.** an uncertain attitude toward others
   - **c.** an advanced college degree
   - **d.** foolish thoughts

3. If you felt self-conscious, you would feel _____.
   - **a.** guilty
   - **b.** proud
   - **c.** nothing because you had fainted
   - **d.** uncomfortably aware of yourself

4. An example of something you might overhaul is a(n) _____.
   - **a.** pet cat
   - **b.** broken bicycle
   - **c.** pile of gravel
   - **d.** unopened bag of new toys

5. If you ponder a decision, you _____.
   - **a.** plant
   - **b.** weather a storm well
   - **c.** do not understand it
   - **d.** consider it carefully

6. People alive today would be most likely to glorify _____.
   - **a.** great leaders from the past
   - **b.** high school dropouts
   - **c.** children under the age of five
   - **d.** computer programmers

7. An example of something that schools might ban is _____.
   - **a.** learning foreign languages
   - **b.** discrimination
   - **c.** reading in the library
   - **d.** riding buses to school

8. A synonym for *self-assured* is _____.
   - **a.** shy
   - **b.** bossy
   - **c.** confident
   - **d.** pleasant

9. You could indicate a direction by _____.
   - **a.** standing still **b.** smiling **c.** pointing **d.** closing your eyes

10. A food company might fortify a cereal by _____.
   - **a.** adding vitamins
   - **b.** advertising it to children
   - **c.** serving it to soldiers
   - **d.** putting prizes in the box

Vocabulary Power

Lesson 33   Using Synonyms

What is your favorite spine-tingling classic—*Frankenstein? Dracula?* People have always loved scary tales that can raise goosebumps. The words in this lesson will help you describe horror stories and people's responses to them.

Word List

aloof	plummet	sinister	tainted
apparition	prophecy	stimulate	unsettling
offend	sequel		

EXERCISE A   Synonyms

Each boldfaced vocabulary word below is paired with a synonym whose meaning you probably know. Think of other words related to the synonym and write them on the line provided. Then, look up the word in a dictionary and write its meaning.

1. **sinister** : evil _____

   Dictionary definition _____

2. **aloof** : reserved _____

   Dictionary definition _____

3. **unsettling** : disturbing _____

   Dictionary definition _____

4. **apparition** : ghost _____

   Dictionary definition _____

5. **plummet** : fall _____

   Dictionary definition _____

6. **stimulate** : excite _____

   Dictionary definition _____

7. **prophecy** : prediction _____

   Dictionary definition _____

8. **offend** : insult _____

   Dictionary definition _____

Vocabulary Power *continued*

9. **tainted** : poisoned _____

   Dictionary definition _____

10. **sequel** : continuation _____

   Dictionary definition _____

EXERCISE B Plot Construction

Here are the titles of four new best-sellers. Use your imagination—and the words from this lesson— to write a brief plot description for each one.

1. *Climbing Mount Everest: The Final Challenge* _____

_____

2. *The Ghost of Tilbury Manor* _____

_____

3. *There's Something About Cats!* _____

_____

4. *The New Millennium and What It Will Mean for You* _____

_____

EXERCISE C Sentence Completion

Circle the word in parentheses that best completes each sentence.

1. The (prophecy, apparition, sequel) to John Queene's first novel is disappointing.

2. She watched the eagle (stimulate, plummet, offend) from its lofty perch.

3. Because someone had tampered with the crime scene, the evidence was regarded as (tainted, aloof, unsettling).

4. The giant oak looked like a ghostly (sequel, apparition, prophecy) in the fog.

5. Saying to yourself, "This could be a bad day," can be a self-fulfilling (apparition, sequel, prophecy) that shapes the way the day will turn out.

Vocabulary Power

Lesson 34   Homophones

Homophones (from the Greek words meaning "same" and "sound") have the same pronunciation but different spellings and meanings. *There, their,* and *they're* are homophones. Although pronounced the same, each word has a different meaning and spelling. In this lesson, you'll learn some often-confused homophones.

Word List			
cite	sight	stationery	vane
complement	site	vain	vein
compliment	stationary		

EXERCISE A Definitions

Look up each word in the dictionary and write its definition on the line.

1. cite _____

2. sight _____

3. site _____

4. vain _____

5. vane _____

6. vein _____

7. complement _____

8. compliment _____

9. stationary _____

10. stationery _____

EXERCISE B Sentence Completion

Write the vocabulary word that best completes the sentence.

1. While out on the ocean in the boat, we were able to _____ several pods of

   whales and a shark or two.

2. In this day of e-mail and faxes, having some nice _____ is a real luxury.

3. Josie's baseball card collection is a perfect _____ to mine because we've collected

   different ones.

Vocabulary Power *continued*

4. We could tell Mr. Rose was angry because the _____ on the side of his neck was bulging out.

5. The pirate captain pointed with his cutlass to the secret _____ of the buried treasure chest.

6. My mom reads a magazine on a book rack attached to her _____ bicycle when she exercises.

7. Andrea is so _____ that she can't pass a mirror without checking her appearance.

8. The lawyer decided to _____ an earlier law case, in which a criminal was freed because the police search had been conducted illegally.

9. Probably the best way to respond to a _____ is to smile and say thank you, or even make a kind remark of your own in return.

10. The rusty weather _____ on the top of the barn was shaped like a rooster and badly needed oiling.

EXERCISE C **Usage**

Read each sentence. If the boldfaced word is used correctly, write *correct* on the line. If not, cross it out and write the correct word above it.

1. The television reporters visited the **cite** of the plane crash and spoke with the survivors.

2. My grandmother always writes to me on light blue **stationery** in dark blue ink.

3. The weather **vain** on top of the cow barn was pointing north, a sign of cold weather to come.

4. I feel that the flavor of ginger snaps is a perfect **complement** to lemon sherbet.

Vocabulary Power

Lesson 35   Borrowed Words

English contains many words that are borrowed from other languages. Some borrowed words are so familiar that you wouldn't imagine that they come from other languages. Others look unusual or different from English words. Dictionaries usually give a borrowed word's history. They also often give its meaning in the original language if different from the meaning used in our language. You will need to look at the explanation of abbreviations used to note the original language. In this lesson, you'll learn some common borrowed words.

Word List

debacle	junta	portfolio	solon
entrepreneur	kosher	rapport	veneer
ersatz	non sequitur		

EXERCISE A Etymology

Look up each borrowed word in a dictionary. Write its meaning in English. Then, fill in the information about its history and original meaning.

1. debacle _____

   From _____ Original Meaning _____

2. solon _____

   From _____ Original Meaning _____

3. entrepreneur _____

   From _____ Original Meaning _____

4. ersatz _____

   From _____ Original Meaning _____

5. rapport _____

   From _____ Original Meaning _____

6. kosher _____

   From _____ Original Meaning _____

7. junta _____

   From _____ Original Meaning _____

8. veneer _____

   From _____ Original Meaning _____

9. non sequitur _____

   From _____ Original Meaning _____

Vocabulary Power *continued*

10. portfolio _____

From _____ Original Meaning _____

EXERCISE B Sentence Completion
Write the word that best completes the sentence.

1. The reporter claimed that there were things going on at city hall that were just not

_____, and she vowed to unmask the wrongdoers.

2. To claim that all football players are good students because they wear protective helmets on the

field is a ridiculous _____.

3. The army was surprised by the attack from the side and suffered a total _____

that led to surrender two months later.

4. The leader of the _____ proclaimed that he would restore order to the streets by

jailing thousands of demonstrators and ordering a strict curfew.

EXERCISE C Television Show Descriptions
Here are the titles of two new television shows. Use your imagination (and at least one vocabulary word from this lesson) to write a short description of each show.

1. "Jason Risk, White House Detective"

_____

_____

_____

2. "I Live a Lie!"

_____

_____

_____

Vocabulary Power

Lesson 36   Using Test-Taking Skills
Analogies

An analogy is a relationship of one thing to another thing. For example, when you say that you love dogs as much as your sister loves cats, you are making an analogy. Your relationship to dogs is the same as your sister's relationship to cats; they're your favorite pets. Analogies are expressed in this way:

> you : dogs :: your sister : cats

Notice that *you* and *your sister* are in the same position in each pair, as are *dogs* and *cats.* Pay careful attention to a word's position in an analogy. The relationships expressed by analogy questions can be of many types. Some of the most common are *antonyms,* or opposites, and *synonyms,* or words that mean the same thing. Others are *differences of degree* (warm : roasting :: cool : freezing); *one of a kind* (ant : insect :: cardinal : bird); *cause and effect* (anger : argument :: hard work : achievement); *parts of a whole* (goalie : team :: drummer: band); *location or description* (basketball player : gymnasium :: student : classroom); *purpose* (knife : cut :: drill : bore); and *person related to skill, tool, or other element* (judge : wisdom :: soldier : bravery). The first step in answering an analogy question is to analyze the relationship so you understand what analogy is being made. Then, look for the choice that best matches the first analogy.

EXERCISE

Circle the letter of the choice that best completes the analogy. Then, write the type of analogy that is being expressed.

1. act : play :: _____
   a. painter : brush   b. actor : TV show   c. chapter : book   d. chair : stack

   Type of Analogy _____

2. warehouse : storage :: _____
   a. university : learning   c. theater : popcorn
   b. store : clothing   d. box : shelf

   Type of Analogy _____

3. studying : good grades :: _____
   a. eating : cafe   c. planting : harvest
   b. familiarity : friends   d. short : height

   Type of Analogy _____

4. trumpet : musical instrument :: _____
   a. ship : navy   c. tree : apple
   b. Mona Lisa : artwork   d. song : singer

   Type of Analogy _____

Vocabulary Power

Review: Unit 8

EXERCISE

Circle the letter of the word that best completes the sentence.

1. The woman carefully removed the important papers from her expensive leather _____.
   a. apparition   **b.** vane   **c.** stationery   **d.** portfolio

2. After his last _____ attempt to climb the rock wall, Russell kicked at a stump in frustration.
   a. vain   **b.** vein   **c.** aloof   **d.** sinister

3. Terry angrily refused to join the group around the fire, remaining alone and _____.
   a. aloof   **b.** sinister   **c.** stationary   **d.** tainted

4. Which authorities did you _____ to support the argument you made in your essay?
   a. sight   **b.** site   **c.** cite   **d.** complement

5. I marveled at the accuracy of the ancient book's _____ about our century.
   a. compliment   **b.** stationery   **c.** prophecy   **d.** non sequitur

6. The seniors' homecoming display could be moved around easily, but the juniors' display was

   _____.
   a. unsettling   **b.** sinister   **c.** tainted   **d.** stationary

7. Underneath where the dark walnut _____ of the table was cracked, you could see a lighter

   wood of some kind.
   a. veneer   **b.** apparition   **c.** sequel   **d.** portfolio

8. Josh's yellow tie was not a very good _____ to his orange shirt and blue jacket.
   a. solon   **b.** rapport   **c.** junta   **d.** complement

9. Marcie rubbed her eyes in disbelief, but the _____ had vanished.
   a. prophecy   **b.** apparition   **c.** stationery   **d.** sequel

10. Have you ever developed a good _____ with someone you've met in an online chat room?
    a. entrepreneur   **b.** solon   **c.** non sequitur   **d.** rapport

Vocabulary Power

Test: Unit 8

PART A

Circle the letter of the word that best completes the sentence.

1. Do you know the _____ of the Super Bowl next year?
   a. sight **b.** vein **c.** cite **d.** site

2. The debate judge cautioned the contestants about making negative remarks that might _____ someone in the audience.
   a. offend **b.** plummet **c.** compliment **d.** complement

3. The punch line of that joke isn't funny, doesn't make sense, and seems like a(n) _____.
   a. compliment **b.** apparition **c.** non sequitur **d.** debacle

4. My opinion is that a _____ to a movie is never as good as the first one.
   a. non sequitur **b.** debacle **c.** sequel **d.** portfolio

5. Samantha's career goal is to become a(n) _____ in the field of telecommunications and run her own business.
   a. entrepreneur **b.** apparition **c.** solon **d.** junta

6. Sometimes I put my school papers in a backpack, sometimes in my notebook, and other times in my _____.
   a. rapport **b.** stationery **c.** apparition **d.** portfolio

7. When arranging flowers, you should choose a vase or holder that will be a good _____ to the flowers you have selected.
   a. veneer **b.** complement **c.** sequel **d.** compliment

8. Our new puppy has had an extremely _____ effect on Dolly, our fourteen-year-old golden retriever.
   a. sinister **b.** tainted **c.** ersatz **d.** unsettling

9. Tim got an after-school job in a _____ store, partly because of his interest in old fountain pens.
   a. stationery **b.** kosher **c.** sinister **d.** stationary

10. The man in the dark cloak standing in the shadows looks _____.
    a. stationery **b.** sinister **c.** stationary **d.** kosher

11. At the antique show, Mom and Dad bought an old weather _____ shaped like a pig.
    a. vain **b.** vein **c.** vane **d.** veneer

Vocabulary Power *continued*

12. A skilled hostage negotiator is trained to develop _____ with a kidnapper.
    a. rapport   **b.** veneer   **c.** complement   **d.** solon

13. Whenever unemployment and inflation rise, the stock market is sure to _____.
    a. offend   **b.** plummet   **c.** sight   **d.** complement

14. Surgeons must be very careful during heart surgery not to damage a _____ or artery.
    a. vane   **b.** vain   **c.** prophecy   **d.** vein

15. Do you know about the ancient _____ of a flood that will destroy the world in 2008?
    a. compliment   **b.** prophecy   **c.** debacle   **d.** sequel

PART B

Circle the letter of the word that belongs with the others.

1. proud, reserved, haughty, _____
   a. aloof   **b.** sinister   **c.** ersatz   **d.** vein

2. poisoned, rotten, spoiled, _____
   a. sinister   **b.** unsettling   **c.** tainted   **d.** ersatz

3. glimpse, glance, view, _____
   a. apparition   **b.** veneer   **c.** prophecy   **d.** sight

4. senator, lawmaker, representative, _____
   a. veneer   **b.** solon   **c.** non sequitur   **d.** vane

5. proper, on the level, fitting, _____
   a. stationary   **b.** ersatz   **c.** kosher   **d.** vain

6. refer, note, quote, _____
   a. sight   **b.** cite   **c.** plummet   **d.** offend

7. fake, substitutive, imitative, _____
   a. kosher   **b.** ersatz   **c.** stationary   **d.** aloof

8. match, fit, completion, _____
   a. complement   **b.** stationery   **c.** sequel   **d.** prophecy

9. government, rulers, leaders, _____
   a. rapport   **b.** portfolio   **c.** apparition   **d.** junta

10. prediction, guess, forecast, _____
    a. apparition   **b.** solon   **c.** prophecy   **d.** stationery

abdicate   ab′də kāt′

abduction   ab dukt′shən

absurd   ab surd′

abundant   ə bun′dənt

acknowledge   ak nol′ij

adept   ə dept′

adherent   ad hēr′ənt

adjourn   ə jurn′

affluent   af′lōō ənt

affront   ə frunt′

agenda   ə jen′də

alliance   ə lī′əns

aloof   ə lōōf′

alternative   ôl tur′nə tiv

anonymous   ə non′ə məs

anthropology   an′thrə pol′ə jē

apathetic   ap′ə thet′ik

apparition   ap′ə rish′ən

arbitrary   är′bə trer′ē

arrogant   ar′ə gənt

askew   ə skū′

assail   ə sāl′

attain   ə tān′

authoritarian   ə thôr′ə tār′ē ən

autonomous   ô ton′ə məs

autopsy   ô′top′sē

awed   ôd

backlog   bak′log′

ban   ban

bastion   bas′chən

belligerent   bə lij′ər ənt

biped   bī′ped′

bisect   bī sekt′

bleak   blēk

byte   bīt

capable   kā′pə bəl

catastrophe   kə tas′trə fē′

certitude   sur′tə tōōd′

chronicle   kron′i kəl

circumnavigate   sur′kəm nav′ə gāt′

cite   sīt

combatant   kəm bat′ənt

commence   kə mens′

compel   kəm pel′

competently   kom′pət ənt lē

complement   kom′plə mənt

complex   kəm pleks′

compliment   kom′plə mənt

comply   kəm plī′

comprehensible   kom′pri hen′sə bəl

consecutive   kən sek′yə tiv

conspicuous   kən spik′ū əs

contradiction   kon′trə dik′shən

cross-reference   krôs′ref′ər əns

cross-section   krôs′sek′shən

crouch   krouch

customize   kus′təm īz

debacle   di bä′kəl

deceptive   di sep′tiv

deflate   di flāt′

defraud   di frôd′

delete   di lēt′

demolish   di mol′ish

demure   di mur′

denigrate   den′ə grāt′

detached   di tacht′

diligent   dil′ə jənt

disclose   dis klōz′

discord   dis′kôrd

disheveled   di shev′əld

disk   disk

dismantle   dis mant′əl

diverse   di vurs′

divert   di vurt′

doctrine   dok′trin

document   dok′yə mənt

dormitory   dôr′mə tôr′ē

dramatize   dram′ə tīz′

dumbfounded   dum′found′id

duration   doo rā′shən

electrify   i lek′trə fī′

eloquence   el′ə kwəns

enclose   en klōz′

endurance   en door′əns

entrepreneur   än′trə prə nur′

envelop   en vəl′əp

envision   en vizh′ən

ersatz   er′zäts

execute   ek′sə kūt′

fabricate   fab′rə kāt′

facilitate   fə sil′ə tāt′

ford   fôrd

format   fôr′mat

fortify   fôr′tə fī′

fortuitous   fôr tōō′ə təs

fragment   frag′mənt

frugal   frōō′gəl

galvanize   gal′və nīz′

gauge   gāj

glorify   glôr′ə fī′

gratitude   grat′ə tōōd′

haggle   hag′əl

haughty   hô′tē

high-minded   hī′mīn′did

hospitable   hos′pi tə bəl

hospitality   hos′pə tal′ə tē

humane   hū mān′

humanoid   hū′mə noid

humid   hū′mid

humility   hū mil′ə tē

hydrophobia   hī′drə fō′bē ə

hysteria   his ter′ē ə

ignoble   ig nō′bəl

illuminate   i lōō′mə nāt′

impediment   im ped′ə mənt

imperative   im per′ə tiv

imperceptible   im′pər sep′tə bəl

imply   im plī′

improbably   im prob′ə blē

impulsive   im pul′siv

incompatible   in′kəm pat′ə bəl

independent   in′di pen′dənt

indicate   in′di kāt′

indifference   in dif′ər əns

indistinct   in′dis tingkt′

infraction   in frak′shən

inhumane   in′hū mān′

initial   i nish′əl

initiative   i nish′ə tiv

integrate   in′tə grāt′

intermediate   in′tər mē′dē it

intervention   in′tər ven′chən

intimate   in′tə mit

intramural   in′trə myoor′əl

intravenous   in′trə vē′nəs

intrigue   in′trēg

invigorating   in vig′ə rāt ing

invincible   in vin′sə bəl

irreversible   ir′i vur′sə bəl

itinerary   ī tin′ər er′ē

jog   jog

junta   hoon′tə

jut   jut

juvenile   jōō′vən əl

kosher   kō′shər

laconic   lə kon′ik

lampoon   lam pōōn′

lapse   laps

lavatory   lav′ə tôr′ē

levitate   lev′ə tāt′

levity   lev′ə tē

loiter   loi′tər

longevity   lon jev′ə tē

lucid   lōō′sid

lurch   lurch

lurk   lurk

luscious   lush′əs

malodorous   mal ō′dər əs

mandate   man′dāt

marshal   mär′shəl

meager   mē′gər

mediate   mē′dē āt′

merge   murj

meticulous   mi tik′yə ləs

microprocessor   mī′krō pros′əs ər

millennium   mi len′ē əm

millisecond   mil′ə sek′ənd

minimal   min′ə məl

monitor   mon′ə tər

monstrosity   mon stros′ə tē

multimedia   mul′ti mē′dē ə′

mutate   mū′tāt

mutation   mū tā′shən

neutralize   nōō′trə līz′

nondescript   non′di skript′

non sequitur   non sek′wi tər

novel   nov′əl

novice   nov′is

obstruction   əb struk′shən

occupant   ok′yə pənt

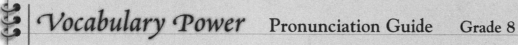

offend   ə fend´

omnivorous   om niv´ər əs

overhang   ō´vər hang´

overhaul   ō´vər hôl´

pact   pakt

pathos   pā´thos

pedestal   ped´əst əl

pentathlon   pen tath´lən

perception   pər sep´shən

perforate   pur´fə rāt´

peripheral   pə rif´ər əl

perish   per´ish

perpetual   pər pech´ōō əl

persistently   pər sis´tənt lē

philosophical   phil´ə sof´i kəl

phobia   fō´bē ə

phonetics   fə net´iks

phonograph   fō´nə graf´

pliant   plī´ənt

plight   plīt

plummet   plum´it

ponder   pon´dər

portfolio   pôrt fō´lē ō´

portray   pôr trā´

postpone   pōst pōn´

preadaptation   prē´ad əp tā´shən

precaution   pri kô´shən

precedence   pres´ə dəns

precipitator   pri sip´ə tāt´ər

precondition   prē´kən dish´ən

prefix   prē´fiks´

premeditated   prē med´ə tāt´id

prevalent   prev´ə lənt

priority   prī ôr´ə tē

prophecy   prof´ə sē

quadruple   kwo drōō´pəl

quell   kwel

rapport   ra pôr´

rebellious   ri bel´yəs

reckless   rek´lis

reconstruct   rē´kən strukt´

recount   ri kount´

recur   ri kur´

refurbish   rē fur´bish

regenerate   ri jen´ə rāt´

rehabilitate   rē´hə bil´ə tāt´

reintegrate   rē in´tə grāt´

remote   ri mōt´

reserve   ri zurv´

resolve   ri zolv´

retain   ri tān´

revive   ri vīv´

rogue   rōg

save   sāv

scowl   skoul

secluded   si klōō´did

sect   sekt

self-assured   self´ə shoord´

self-conscious   self´kon´shəs

semiannual   sem´ē an´ū əl

semicircle   sem´ē sur´kəl

sequel   sē´kwəl

serene   sə rēn´

serenity   sə ren´ə tē

sibling   sib´ling

sight   sīt

significant   sig nif´i kənt

simultaneous   sī´məl tā´nē əs

single-minded   sing´gəl mīn´did

sinister   sin´is tər

site   sīt

socialize   sō´shə līz´

solon   sō´lən

sophisticated   sə fis´tə kā´tid

specimen   spes´ə mən

spectacle   spek´tə kəl

stationary   stā´shə ner´ē

stationery   stā´shə ner´ē

stimulate   stim´yə lāt´

sullen   sul´ən

summon   sum´ən

superb   soo purb´

surpass   sər pas´

tainted   tānt´id

taunt   tônt

tempo   tem´pō

temporary   tem´pə rer´ē

testimony   tes´tə mō´nē

token   tō´kən

tranquillity   trang kwil´ə tē

transfix   trans fiks´

transmission   trans mish´ən

trinkets   tring´kits

trite   trīt

unabashed   un´ə basht´

uncomprehendingly   un kom´pri hend´ing lē

underscore   un´dər skôr´

undertake   un´dər tāk´

unidirectional   ū nə di rek´shən əl

unify   ū´nə fī´

universal   ū´nə vur´səl

unseemly   un sēm´lē

unsettling   un set´ling

unsound   un sound´

urban   ur´bən

urbanite   ur´bə nīt´

vacant   vā´kənt

vague   vāg

vain   vān

valiant   val´yənt

valid   val´id

vane   vān

varied   vār´ēd

vast   vast

vein   vān

veneer   vi nēr´

verbal   vur´bəl

vibrant   vī´brənt

vigorous   vig´ər əs

vindictive   vin dik´tiv

virtue   vur´cho̅o̅

vivid   viv´id

wholesome   hōl´səm

woe   wō

zoom   zo̅o̅m